Praise for *The Imagination Matrix*

"*The Imagination Matrix* is an exceptional gift. Stephen Aizenstat provides the essential tools to live a life with richer meaning and awe. The reader will be immediately transported to a life of wonder and possibilities and be renewed in their dedication to a positive future. The timing of this book could not be more ideal and relevant."

Jennifer Freed, PhD
author of the bestseller *A Map to Your Soul*

"*The Imagination Matrix* offers portals of awareness through which each reader can find their inner code of life and their living core of creative imagination. This radical shift in consciousness transforms individuals and communities, and also supports the entire planet."

Michael Meade
author of *Awakening the Soul*

"Reading *The Imagination Matrix* gives us access to our capacities to cocreate the higher dream that is longing to come into existence. The practices and gifts of this extraordinary book offer training and participation to redeem the unread vision of the higher dream. *The Imagination Matrix* is *the* essential reading for those who want to bring profoundly new ways of being and doing into this world and time."

Jean Houston, PhD
principal founder of the Human Potential Movement,
coauthor of the Future Humans Trilogy

"In *The Imagination Matrix*, Stephen Aizenstat assembles a wealth of sources, as well as his own reflections on stuckness versus creativity, and offers a multiphase plan for a renewed relationship to that generative source within each of us. The capacity for reimagining the materials of daily life is inherent but often blocked by the inner tyrants of complexes and routinized life. This book will ask the reader to break some of those restraints and open to the insurgent images that reframe our dilemmas and that wish expression through us in the world."

James Hollis, PhD

Jungian analyst and author of multiple books, most recently *A Life of Meaning*

"Imagination is different from knowledge; it is the knowledge of the heart. Through the Imagination Matrix, you can enter and feel the realms of deep imagination, live an imagination-centered life, and access Imaginal Healing. What a magnetic calling, as the Imagination Matrix is alive in each of us."

Professor Heyong Shen

Jungian analyst; dean of the Institute of Analytical Psychology, City University of Macau; author of *Chinese Cultural Psychology* and eleven other volumes

"Stephen Aizenstat is unquestionably one of the great leaders in the field of deep imagination and dreaming of our generation. His work as a Dream Tender and as the founder of Pacifica Graduate Institute has profoundly changed the lives of thousands of people. And now there is this book, which will give many more the opportunity to tap into the healing creativity of the involuntary imagination as it establishes itself around us constantly in the endless stories it spontaneously spins. Dive in with this experienced guide of souls and find your way into the creative genius that surrounds us day and night."

Robert Bosnak, PsyA

Jungian psychoanalyst, originator of Embodied Imagination®, author of *Red Sulphur*

"*The Imagination Matrix* by Stephen Aizenstat is an imaginal companion that everyone should have. It is a true gift to the world that activates and calls upon our creative genius for taking on the greatest challenges of our time, infusing our lives, work, and relationships with meaning, story, and the powers of the imaginal realms of consciousness. Through it we learn to partner the essences of the Four Quadrants—Earth, Mind, Machine, and Universe—supported by cutting-edge research and breakthrough practices and applications from the fields of earth sciences, depth psychology, new technologies, and cosmology.

This powerful guidebook will significantly up-level your life and work in ways seen and unseen. Aizenstat's brilliant storytelling evokes your Curious Mind and guides you home to your beloved Soul Companions, as you discover how to empower each other and answer our deeper calling for being.

The Imagination Matrix prepares us for the massive transformations that are required from us at this time and in ways that rekindle our Imaginal Play, invite fun, increase joy and wonder, and deepen our love for life, Gaia, and each other."

Anneloes Smitsman, PhD
founder of EARTHwise Centre, coauthor of the Future Humans Trilogy

"A marvelous journey into the worlds of imagination! Through stories, practical examples, and supportive ideas, Stephen Aizenstat leads you to connect with the creative and healing powers of imagination. Become friends with your Soul Companions, and go on an adventure of a lifetime!"

Machiel Klerk
founder of Jung Platform, author of *Dream Guidance*, psychotherapist

"A long-awaited, new, wise, and soulful offering by the creator of Dream Tending, *The Imagination Matrix* offers a passionate vision for fulfilling our human potentials. Stephen Aizenstat brings a twenty-first century understanding of depth psychology into a rich and complex engagement with the world through a disciplined cultivation of the imagination. Using a contemporary re-visioning of the four elements, we are offered a set of salient tools for animating and enlivening our world, including its material, technological, ecological, and spiritual dimensions. Written with an utterly charming and enchanting narrative style, this book also conveys profound wisdom through stories that open our minds in a practical and immediately applicable manner. Engaging with this book will transform you."

Joe Cambray, PhD

IAAP past-president, Pacifica Graduate Institute

"Stephen Aizenstat's *Imagination Matrix* reawakens our Indigenous spiritual roots! This book is simply magic!"

André McCray, MFT

Black Dreams Matter Project

"A bountiful journey spiraling vertically down into the deep dig of curiosity, returning upward through imagination. The interconnective process that Stephen Aizenstat created prepares and illuminates a path to healing through entering the Story-Web. An easy and engaging read, this book offers a journey into depth psychology and forwards the reader, using portals, to their destiny via the Imagination Matrix. Don't miss the chance to find YOU!"

Thyonne Gordon, PhD

business profit strategist, The Thyonne Group

"If you want to learn how to creatively engage your imagination, there is no greater teacher than Stephen Aizenstat. He is a wizard of the wit, an emperor of the intuition, a magus of the imagination who can show you the way into the mystical, magical land that lies deep within your mind. Through inspiring personal stories; clear, thoughtful instruction; and powerful, effective exercises, you will learn to 'tap into and activate the Imagination Matrix to innovate new outcomes, evolve real-world solutions, and nurture your well-being.'"

Michael W. Taft

author of *The Mindful Geek* and *Nondualism*, coauthor of *Ego*

"*The Imagination Matrix* by Stephen Aizenstat invites the reader into a world of possibilities in our twenty-first century, bridging old consciousness with new. Through his writing, he has created a practical structure that joyfully provides us with support for the inner spirit. Experiential moments described in the book awaken the mind and engage the soul through a Curious Mind concept that leads to Innate Genius in practice. We are given everything that we require to truly live, fully embodied while engaged with the world. Loneliness is transformed, love is possible, and generosity becomes the gift of the individual to all that exists on our planet. Aizenstat offers us a rich path for inner reflection that helps light the way for others. This is truly a book that teaches wisdom and guidance for a most enticingly rich inner life. *The Imagination Matrix* offers heartfelt ways to deepen the consciousness of mind, body, and spirit."

Fanny Brewster, PhD

author of *Race and the Unconscious*

"The Imagination Matrix is a prescient and thought-provoking framework at the convergence point of technology and imagination. As our realities become blurred and boundaries are redefined, the Four Quadrants serve as a guide in maximizing creativity and human potential in ways we can only yet begin to imagine."

Rob Patrick

CTO and entrepreneur

"Stephen Aizenstat has a knack for accessing and connecting to the young person in all of us. Our youth have never been in greater need of connection, and the ideas, exercises, and lessons in *The Imagination Matrix* provide a unique, creative path for young people to develop and solidify the innate intelligence within us. It is a rarity to find a book equally accessible to young people and adults; Aizenstat has accomplished this and more."

Myka Hanson, PhD

founder of Teen Forward

"At the core, this book is a life raft for the twenty-first century. It is a manual for a brand-new, paradigm-shifting, and necessary way of seeing the world. Without minimizing the problems facing our culture, Stephen Aizenstat teaches his readers how to access a deeper level of imagination and how this opens us up to healing, inner support, and a sense of authentic interconnectedness. It will, without a doubt, help countless writers and storytellers connect to a deeper, mythic quality in their work and tell meaningful stories that point the way toward a hopeful future."

Louise Rosager

executive producer and writing coach, The Unlimited Writer and
Wake Up and Dream

"What does it mean to be human in a digital world? The research increasingly points toward a future that is less about what we know and more about the capacity we can build for imagination and innovation. But we know we can't get there in stressed-out beta brain. We need skills and resources to tap into our own Innate Genius that can only be revealed through alpha and theta brain wave states. In other words, the solutions to our challenges today cannot be found outside of ourselves but rather within our 'reciprocal relationship between Imaginal Intelligence and body wisdom.' Steve Aizenstat maps a path through a frenetic and distracted world, toward connection and creativity, in this important book, *The Imagination Matrix*."

Carol Grojean, PhD

flow and peak performance coach; board member, Academy
of Imagination; former senior director at Microsoft

"Not for nothing did the poet Wallace Stevens refer to the imagination as 'the necessary angel' that allows us to 'see the world again.' Steve Aizenstat's book is in that tradition; it reminds us of the transformative power of the imagination, its power to creatively produce something entirely new rather than merely reproduce what has gone before. Without such a book, the imagination is in danger of becoming extinct. This book gives the imagination the new lease on life it urgently needs to help us understand how things *might* be."

Lionel Corbett, MD

author of *Psyche and the Sacred*, *The Religious Function of the Psyche*, and eight other books and edited collections; certified Jungian analyst; faculty member, Pacifica Graduate Institute

"Stephen Aizenstat's new book furthers and deepens his internationally acclaimed Dream Tending method for working with our dream life. His new book reveals that on our individual journey we are not alone. Through his guidance we learn to look more closely at our life's plot and notice where aids and mentors are very much part of the fabric of our fictions. *The Imagination Matrix* is in the richest sense a guidebook. And its weave successfully joins the realms of imagination, perception, self-trust, myth, history, and depth psychology into a new form—one that can inform and transform individuals, assisting them in becoming more conscious of their own wisdom story."

Dennis Patrick Slattery, PhD

distinguished professor emeritus in mythological studies at Pacifica Graduate Institute; author of, most recently, *The Way of Myth* and *The Fictions in Our Convictions*

"Stephen Aizenstat surfaces the hidden gifts of the horrific and the broken. He teaches how to befriend the autonomous, living images of dream and imagination so that they can be welcomed as Soul Companions. These practices support activating the portals of imagination, liberating and illuminating healing and transformative creative energies for the regeneration of earth, soma, and soul. This vibrant volume offers training that reclaims and restores, orienting to the emerging possible. In a time when the Earth is on fire, working with the Imagination Matrix offers fresh approaches to innovate Earth-enhancing possibilities while sustaining greater resilience, courage, and inspiration for the long haul. Working with the Imagination Matrix brings fresh allies and support for the world-healing work before us."

Marna Hauk, PhD

coeditor of *Vibrant Voices* and *Community Climate Change Education*; associate director, doctoral program in Visionary Practice and Regenerative Leadership, Southwestern College and New Earth Institute

"Like the warm California beaches it was written on, *The Imagination Matrix* beckons us to play. Aizenstat gives voice to a lifelong journey of opening to curiosity. Through well-illustrated core concepts and exercises, he directs us toward participation with the inner life inside of us. Viva psyche!"

Gary S. Bobroff

founder of Jungian Online and JUNG Archademy

"A tender of dreams and a mender of souls, Stephen Aizenstat reimagines imagination from the playa at Burning Man to the halls of the United Nations. Delivering just what the world needs most in these times of psychological distress and planetary trauma, using his dynamic therapeutic approach, Aizenstat shows his readers how they can live an imagination-centered life and access the deep wisdom of imaginal realms, putting them in touch with rich inner resources that nourish consciousness, heal individual hearts, and inspire fresh meaning in diverse communities and identities."

Frank N. McMillan

author of *Finding Jung*, cofounder of Academy of Imagination

"For those interested in the future of leadership, Steve has favored us with his breakthrough treatment of the nature and role of imagination and innovation. The direction of leadership thinking has been transforming from the outdated, hierarchical 'machine model' metaphor into understanding the role of individual and collective imagination and creativity of the team. Steve has laid the completing segment of that bridge in his comprehensive program, describing new concepts such as the Imagination Matrix, Four Quadrants, the Curious Mind, and many other aspects of cultivating the deep imagination with life-changing benefits. It seems that his concept of Imaginal Intelligence is destined to match or exceed the contributions of Emotional Intelligence that preceded it. Enjoy every page."

Thomas Steding, PhD

author of *Real Teams Win*, coauthor of *Built on Trust*

"These new teachings and activities are essential in firing imagination, unlocking innate curiosity, and revealing the splendor of both the tangible world and the creative realm. Those of us living ordinary lives can find in these pages simple steps toward discovering the extraordinary just beneath the threshold of our awareness."

Randal Lea, MA, LADAC
Cumberland Heights Foundation; adjunct faculty,
Southwestern College and New Earth Institute

"These pages are an illuminated manuscript in which Stephen sparks our visionary selves through sharing his lifelong harvest with generosity and wonder. He reminds us that our dreams give us direct access to the landscape of myth, magic, and possibility. This realm is replete with wisdom and healing, and spending time there makes for a richly creative, spirited life. Grounded in practical applications, Stephen shows us that the reclamation of the potency alive in the imaginal realms has a simple gateway, and that is the realm of dreams. Curiosity and openness are all we need to walk through the door, and an oracular way of seeing, being, and living is what we find on the other side. The work contained in these pages can feel like play. And yet, it is some of the most powerful medicine for a world of humans who so need to feel a deeper sense of belonging and connection. The methods herein are not only healing; they are uplifting. Gratitude to Stephen for his masterful, lifelong contribution as an emissary from the realm of dreams. Clearly, the dream figures chose well."

Karla Refoxo
The Tulku Oracle

"AI . . . ChatGPT . . . Bard . . . Stephen Aizenstat's *The Imagination Matrix* is more than a *road map* to human survival in this sometimes-frightening digital world. Through his magical storytelling skills, Aizenstat leads us on a journey, step by step, from the Dig to the Curious Mind to the Imagination Matrix, where we discover the *power of being human* in the technological playground in which we live. Supported with real-life events from his professional experience as a renowned psychologist and founder of Pacifica Graduate Institute, Aizenstat introduces us to our Soul Companions, who heighten our imagination and expand our creativity. We learn not to fear the machine but to develop a successful cocreative relationship with the machine, the technology. We are given lessons from the desert's Burning Man and Australia's goanna lizard. Most important, we are given the path to grow our own Innate Genius, from the inside out.

The Imagination Matrix belongs to all of us, from elementary teachers and children to code creators to parents to corporate executives and anyone who desires a more creative and fulfilling life in our highly evolving universe."

Linda Hayes

president, Linda Hayes Consulting LLC; board member, Academy of Imagination

"Having had the pleasure of studying the skills and concepts in *The Imagination Matrix* with Stephen the last five years, I can say that it has been a life-changing experience. Not only has it helped me to heal deep personal wounds, but it has given me an essential daily practice that keeps my mental health on an even keel, my creativity a portal to flow from, and a deep sense of connection with Soul. The Imagination Matrix does for the imagination what his pioneering Dream Tending work did for dreams—opens up a vast inner world to access creativity, healing, and communing deeply with the collective unconscious. It reveals the true potential of the human mind and is a balm for the chaotic times we find ourselves in."

Kelly Carlin

founder, Humans on the Verge

"Reading this book, one feels the drum beat of story and the riveting energy emergent in embodied imaginal practice. The wisdom of the ancestors gathers in the experiential exercises Aizenstat skillfully provides as guides and containers. Aizenstat invites us to be vitally present with dream, story, figure, and creature. His compassionate ethos stands in deep abiding relationship with the spirit of land, rock, and house. This complements the grounded and grounding clinical skills that one may develop and thoughtfully apply to one's own engagement with the imaginal and emergent. Give this book as a gift to your practice. May it be humbly received."

Willow Young
president of the board of directors, Opus Archives

THE IMAGINATION
MATRIX

Also by Stephen Aizenstat

Dream Tending: Awakening to the Healing Power of Dreams

*Imagination and Medicine: The Future of Healing
in an Age of Neuroscience*

THE IMAGINATION
MATRIX

How to Access the
Greatest Power You Have for
Creativity, Connection, and Purpose

STEPHEN AIZENSTAT, Ph.D.

sounds true
BOULDER, COLORADO

Sounds True
Boulder, CO

Published 2023

Book design by Charli Barnes

Printed in Canada

BK06539

Library of Congress Cataloging-in-Publication Data

Names: Aizenstat, Stephen, author.
Title: The imagination matrix : how to access the greatest power you have
    for creativity, connection, and purpose / by Stephen Aizenstat, PhD.
Description: Boulder, CO : Sounds True, 2023. | Includes bibliographical
    references.
Identifiers: LCCN 2023003247 (print) | LCCN 2023003248 (ebook) | ISBN
    9781649630025 (hardback) | ISBN 9781649630032 (ebook)
Subjects: LCSH: Creative ability. | Creation (Literary, artistic, etc.) |
    Creative thinking. | Imagination. | Dream interpretation.
Classification: LCC BF408 .A36 2023 (print) | LCC BF408
    (ebook) | DDC 153.3/5--dc23/eng/20230203
LC record available at https://lccn.loc.gov/2023003247
LC ebook record available at https://lccn.loc.gov/2023003248

10 9 8 7 6 5 4 3 2 1

Contents

Introduction: Remembering the Source Code of Imagination   I

Ritual of Intention   II

Part 1: Internal Discovery

Chapter 1: Following Curiosity   15

Foundational Template: Relaxing into Breath   21

Foundational Template: Opening the Curious Mind   24

Chapter 2: Journeying in the Realms of Deep Imagination   27

The Dig   29

Foundational Template: The Descent   32

Foundational Template: The Return   35

Chapter 3: Soul Companions   39

Foundational Template: Receiving Teachings from Soul Companions   42

Foundational Template: Illuminating Your Supportive Soul Companions   46

Foundational Template: Transmuting Your Shadow Companions   58

Chapter 4: The Four Quadrants of the Imagination Matrix   63

Working with Quadrant 1: Earth   66
Working with Quadrant 2: Mind   68
Working with Quadrant 3: Machine   70
Working with Quadrant 4: Universe   72

Chapter 5: Imaginal Intelligence   75

Receiving Insights from the Quadrants: IQ4   78
Increasing Theta: Eyes Open/Attention Outward   81
Increasing Theta: Eyes Closed/Attention Inward   82

Chapter 6: Discovering Your Innate Genius   89

Foundational Template: Cultivating Innate Genius   93
Expanding Your Modes of Perception: The Quick Shift Protocol   96
Commitment to Yourself: Actualizing Your Innate Genius   97

Part 2: In the World

Chapter 7: Utilizing the Imagination Matrix System   101

Activating the Curious Mind: The Quick Shift Protocol   102

Chapter 8: Living the Imagination-Centered Life   121

Illuminated Consciousness: The Quick Shift Protocol   124
Inviting the Third Body into Your Relationships   129
Foundational Template: Incubating Creativity in the Workplace 133
Commitment to Yourself: Embodying Ensouled Stewardship   135

Chapter 9: Imaginal Healing   137

Soul Companion the Inner Physician: Four Steps for Illumination 138
Foundational Template: Opening Perception for Imaginal Healing 142
Accessing Imaginal Healing: The Quick Shift Protocol   148

Chapter 10: Keeping Our Humanity in a Technological World   151

Soul Companion the Monster in the Machine: Four Steps to
Transmutation   157
Foundational Template: Welcoming Imaginal Figures into the
Family System   160
Feeling Overtaken by Tech: The Quick Shift Protocol   167
Accessing Flow: The Quick Shift Protocol   169

Chapter 11: The Story-Web   173

Foundational Template: Evoking the Story-Web   176
Foundational Template: Opening to the Story-Web   185
Commitment to Yourself: Accessing the World Through the
Story-Web   190

Epilogue: The Pull of the Future   193

Ritual of Service   195

Gratitudes   197
Glossary   201
Notes   207
Recommended Reading   221
About the Author   227

Remembering the Source Code of Imagination

"We must let go of the life we have planned,
so as to accept the one that is waiting for us."

Joseph Campbell

If ever there was a time and a place to reconnect with imagination, that place is here and that time is now. Humanity stands at a crossroads, one direction leading to worse destruction, the other to the endless possible. Your contribution could help tip the balance to propel humanity forward to its better future. A pathway exists for you to make this contribution. The methods I offer in this book have helped thousands of people around the world—people just like you—tap into and activate the Imagination Matrix to innovate new outcomes, evolve real-world solutions, and nurture their well-being. In the following chapters, I describe how to gain access to this source code of imagination within each of us.

We are born with a living blueprint, the essential design to evolve our imagination. Each of us enters the world with the capacity to make creative leaps of consciousness and quantum leaps in learning.

Our discerning brains and our sensate bodies are built for imaginative exploration. The first sparks or hints of this biological instinct emerge soon after birth. Studies have shown that when babies play, they are engaged in creative exploration, which is the basis of imagination. As babies experiment with new sights, sounds, and activities and solve simple problems, their imaginations develop.[1] Throughout your lifetime, imaginative play is foundational to emotional and social development.

Traditionally, *imagination* refers to the ability to form a picture in your mind of something not previously seen or experienced. Every one of us has access to this inner aptitude. If you are feeling out of touch with your imagination, that's okay. This book offers a framework for you to access the generative power within that is waiting to be known. Your imagination holds the ideas and images that you can use to impact the world of today and that of tomorrow.

Most of the time, your thoughts are governed by your rational mind, separated from this creative force. And for good reason. Humanity has used the discipline of deductive reasoning to make tremendous advances in science, technology, medicine, architecture, and government. These disciplines, in many ways, have contributed greatly to well-being. Modern education supports task-oriented thinking with content-based learning, which emphasizes finding solutions to problems in the most efficient ways possible.

However, the Imagination Matrix offers another pathway to generative solutions. Many sectors of contemporary culture are placing new value on the role of an expansive imagination. This shift in consciousness is impacting individuals, communities, and even how we care for the planet. From the imagination-based curriculum that Harvard Business School instituted in 2011 to creativity incubators embedded in many corporations, from image-centered psychological-treatment programs to the application of Imaginal thinking in urban planning, the infusion of imagination is revitalizing the ways we conduct business and interact with one another. The trailblazers are people like you:

the seekers, the creatives, the workers, the dreamers, the doers. You who are willing and ready to tap into a collective purpose that is vital, vibrant, and resonant in the world of today.

I see and feel the force of imagination pushing forward every day when I teach, lead workshops, consult with corporations, or confer with policymakers at the United Nations. In the classroom, teaching platforms as well as content-delivery systems are changing at an accelerating pace. Learning is no longer limited to memorization and rote regurgitation of facts. Students are challenged to utilize their Imaginal capacities to make conceptual extrapolations and innovative advancements. Technology offers access to an unprecedented array of field studies, visual demonstrations, and historical backgrounds from which to develop their concepts.

In my environmental work at the United Nations, I see the same dynamics at work. Traditional modes of perception and conventional problem-solving tools are not applicable to a rapidly changing ecosystem. The Earth Charter International, the design of which I took part in, is an example of this kind of imagination-centered undertaking. In order to move toward a more just, supportable, and peaceful world with world leaders and experts in environmental-policy formation, we put together a plan inspired by imagination for legislating sustainability that adheres to sixteen agreed-upon principles. The charter has been formally endorsed by the United Nations Educational, Scientific, and Cultural Organization (UNESCO)[3] and integrated into pioneering international educational initiatives. As part of the UN's Sustainable Development Goals,[4] millions of youth organizations, civic groups, municipalities, and nations have committed to it.[5]

It is auspicious that just when we have the need, a massive shift in our Imaginal capacities is occurring. You can see new models for cocreating environmental change and for doing business arising in urban planning, for example. Smart cities like Oslo, Norway, use new technologies to counter climate change by generating renewable energy through smart grids and electric vehicles. The architecture of the city is grounded in the principles of sustainability—the sympathetic relationship between the human made and the nature made. And you can see it in the ways in which companies such as Chapul Farms are increasing biodiversity in agriculture in order to cultivate a more sustainable, resilient, and secure food system for the planet. At their "innovation center" in McMinnville, Oregon, Chapul Farms imagined how to use insects and the microbial ecosystems they nurture to restore soil health, eliminate organic waste, and produce a nutrient-rich and healthy food system. Another example is the visionary work of Winona LaDuke (Anishinaabe) as the founder of the White Earth Land Recovery Project, which exemplifies the possibilities of regenerative community development and agriculture twined with language and cultural resurgence.

I believe this global emphasis on growing our Imaginal capacities will pull human evolution into the abundant future on a collective and individual level. This is because the imagination moving through you has a potent life of its own. However, to unlock its power, you need to unplug from the overdrive of contemporary life and create the time and space to listen within. Slowing down, separating from the to-do list, and quieting the busy mind provide space for something other to express itself. In this state of quiet, the *Curious Mind*, spontaneous imagination has the room to present on its own behalf. Taking just twenty minutes each day and quieting down invites the imagination—which is always moving through you, just below the surface of your awareness—to make an appearance. The material contained in these pages guides you into another way of listening.

How to Use This Book

The Imagination Matrix is designed to help you access the deepest capacities of your imagination. The book offers a pathway to the Imagination Matrix and the generative realms waiting to be known. Each chapter is grounded with research, case studies, and illustrative stories.

The imagination loves to be met in the way of stories. Each chapter also includes interactive exercises to help you bring the power of the Imagination Matrix into your life. These activities are designed to draw you into personal reflection and playful consideration, and they can and should be adapted to support individual circumstances and abilities. In my years of teaching and lecturing, I have found this toggling between the conceptual and the experiential to be the most profound way of engaging the great mysteries of the human experience.

This book invites your interaction with it. You can read it in the order in which it is laid out. But also feel free to skip ahead or go back, dipping into the stories and exercises as needed for inspiration. While moving through these concepts, feel free to mark up the pages. Add notes to the margins. Make it your own. I also recommend keeping a separate journal, your own special place for recording your insights, dreams, drawings, and imaginings. As your imagination opens, stories will begin flowing through your direct experiences. When you describe what you are seeing or feeling in words or by drawing, you are giving the imagination actuality.

The book unfolds in eleven short chapters. Each builds upon the previous one. I use a new language, a new way of writing, to guide you back to the imaginative mind and invite you to think differently. You will discover many new terms while reading; you can refer to the glossary in the back for any clarification that may be helpful. The book is constructed in two parts, beginning with internal work and then moving to external and real-world applications.

Part 1: The Internal Discovery

The book starts by leading you into a shift in consciousness that is the basic tool necessary to begin the journey within. The Western world is familiar with the practice of meditation as a tool to enhance self-discovery sourced from living wisdom traditions in Egypt, China, India, and elsewhere.[6] Where meditation might focus on a particular word or sound or the notion of the empty mind, our work begins with opening the Curious Mind. This form of active awareness engages with realms seen and unseen. We then deepen this engagement with the process I call *the Dig*, in which we excavate down into the realms of the Imagination Matrix. In this inward journey, we will encounter elemental and Imaginal figures who offer support and guidance. I call these figures *Soul Companions*, as they become internal compasses whose strengths and characteristics accompany us as we step through the portal into the Imagination Matrix. In this stage of the journey, we encounter the forces found in the Four Quadrants: *Earth*, *Mind*, *Machine*, and *Universe*. It is here you will be given the tools to discover and enhance your Imaginal intelligence and your Innate Genius.

These terms, along with others, might be new to you. We will take the time to unpack the subtleties and complexities of new concepts as we move forward.

Part 2: In the World

Part 2 reveals how to apply the skills and insights that you have acquired in part 1. It offers practical ways you can utilize the Imagination Matrix System at work, at home, and in building an Imagination-Centered Life.

This part begins by introducing the Imagination Matrix System, a problem-solving engine, and explaining how to use it. You uncover how it can assist in practices of Imaginal Healing and well-being, both psychologically and physiologically. In doing so, questions are raised about how to keep your humanity in an increasingly technological world. It is here that your journey comes full circle. As the Imagination Matrix is sparked by the multiplicity of stories, the *Story-Web* that underpins everything is revealed. It is in this Story-Web, connecting past to present, that you will feel the pull of the future, your purpose, and your destiny waiting to be discovered.

What Is the Imagination Matrix?

The Imagination Matrix is the creative force moving through all forms of being. It is ever present and exists below, betwixt, and between the surfaces of everyday experience. It seems that we in the modern age have forgotten how to access this transformational internal technology. The noise and frenzy of our busy lives block this natural attunement with the universal and with ourselves. When you experience the Illumination that is generated from the Imagination Matrix, you are able to see the shimmering of what exists between people or the luminosity between creatures and landscapes. You glimpse the radiance of imagination that surrounds and permeates all that is around us. This occurs not when you push, but when you let go of the need to know, the drive to succeed, and the will to control. You, and each of us, must relearn to kindle our sense of wonder—that joyous feeling of being alive, here, now. You can't be depressed or controlling when you are in wonder.[7]

Wonder is something that exists just behind the veil of the familiar. As a child you spent many hours in imaginative play, which I call *Imaginal Play*, crafting drawings and stories. It was as natural as breathing. Children are far more in tune with these conversations inherent to all creatures and things.

But as we grow, most people lose their connection to the Imagination Matrix. Parents and teachers train us to put away Imaginal Play, to get on with the concerns and necessities of life. Yet, between the cracks of the everyday, the source code lives. You may not be paying direct attention, but faint whispers of it arise in your life. A daydream visits as you gaze toward the horizon. A night dream interrupts your sleep as you lie in bed. An out-of-the-box idea pushes through just when you find yourself caught in an unworkable situation. And you take the time to listen.

Your Curious Mind

Engaging wonder in the Imagination Matrix is not as much about *what* you see and hear as it is about *how* you perceive and listen. *Seeing* with an aesthetic eye toward what is fascinating opens perception into the deeper mysteries. *Listening* with a receptive ear for what is captivating opens hearing into the inner rhythms. *Opening* to a Curious Mind accesses the epic stories within and without all creation. These moments of enlightened curiosity companion you. Linear space and time yield to something more. You might wonder, *Am I hearing the through lines of the source code itself?*

This experience of the Imagination Matrix might sound esoteric, even fanciful. Actually, it is more embodied than whimsical. In more than forty years of working closely with colleagues and mentors such as Joseph Campbell, Jean Houston, Marion Woodman, James Hillman, and many others in the academy, I have had the privilege to confer with some of the greatest minds of the previous generation. Meeting, sharing stories, and collaborating with international dreamers has also nourished this work, including with Chinese Jungian analyst and scholar Professor Heyong Shen. Briefly yet meaningfully, I interacted with Aboriginal dreamers Bill Neijdie and Bill Harvey. In Hawai'i, I talked story with Lulu, a kahuna of the dreaming. This work takes further inspiration from experiences with sustainability and seed-saving activist Dr. Vandana Shiva and community organizers Dolores Huerta and the late Cesar Chavez. The work of these foundational thinkers sets the stage for and opens the doors to our consideration of a matrix of imagination. I draw upon and build on their works, along with those of Carl Jung. I now offer my concepts to the canon based upon contemporary research and the evolving circumstances of our times.

From the masterwork of Jung comes his extraordinary contribution to the field of Western psychology: the concept of the collective unconscious. For Jung and those who followed in the depth psychological tradition, the psyche consists of more than person-centered consciousness and development. Archetypal images found in cross-cultural myths and stories are present in personal psychological experience and appear in dreams and fantasy. With an autonomy of their own, these Imaginal figures and motifs shape behavior and offer insight into universal teachings. From Jung comes the idea of "the one and the many": that the mind is more than ego, more than a singular, rational operating system. The consciousness of mind consists of the many selves.

James Hillman extended the work of Jung. For Hillman, images are phenomenal, soul bodies with Imaginal presence and pulse. Hillman offered ways of seeing the imagination in its dynamic presentation. The nature-made as well as the human-made are ensouled with inner qualities of their own. Machines also have an Imaginal presence. When we open our perception, all creation presents itself to the imagination. We can cultivate the capacity to befriend, even learn from, these images that visit psychic life. Marion Woodman's work introduced the elemental teaching that body and psyche are inseparable. The way to healing lies in finding a connection between body and soul, earth and spirit.

My work synthesizes the contributions of these seminal thinkers, along with findings in the fields of philosophy, new physics, and more, into a new vision for understanding yourself and others. It is also informed by Indigenous cultures who have explored the universe of consciousness consisting of an Illuminated cosmos above (the movements of planets and stars) and an animated world below (the interrelated networks of animals and landscapes). The Imagination Matrix System brings together these multidimensional states of awareness (Earth, Mind, Machine, and Universe). When these states of awareness are integrated with information systems, communication networks, human curiosity, and wonder, a sort of magic occurs.

In my work, I have developed particularized curricula and implemented specialized training regimens proven to access the meta-intelligence of the Imagination Matrix so that you can live a more attuned and awakened life. You are on a journey into the unknown, taking up the torch along with existing and past generations.

To begin a journey, you need to have a destination in mind. When you travel in the physical world, you might choose to go to a place that has meaning to you. When you journey inward, you connect to an Imaginal destination (such as a memory or a dream) or an emotional experience. This book will guide and support you in your Imaginal adventure.

The success of any journey depends, in large part, on how you prepare. I have found that the getting-ready phase of journeying is not only vital but, indeed, part of the journey itself. Rituals of preparation—the praxis of incubation—precede most rites of passage, from the familiar (known) to the vastly expansive unfamiliar (unknown). Traveling requires a well-intentioned mindset, a shift in psychospiritual orientation, and the need to put your house in order. Incubation involves writing down your packing list (the tools and provisions you will need): supplies include restorative breathing techniques, self-nurturing writing methods, and creative arts processes. Similar to astronauts preparing for travel to outer space, you need to assemble all the resources to sustain your journey. Then, you must shift out of the rational mind, which is focused on doing, and open your Curious Mind to the Imaginal process. This change of perception readies you for the adventure to what Joseph Campbell called "the outer reaches of inner space."[8]

The Imagination Matrix is alive in each of us. We experience the matrix as a kind of inheritance, a bequest from the beginning. With the excitement of an anticipated destination now sparking through mind and body, it is time to get started. Let's set our intentions for our journey together into the mystery and the magic of the Imagination Matrix and the powerful energies found there.

Ritual of Intention

Find a quiet place that helps you center.

    —Locate yourself in a safe space in your home or in the natural landscape.

Light a candle, actually or Imaginally. Repeat to yourself three times, "What is being asked of me?"

    —Let each time deepen the resonance of the ask.

Listen without judgment. Open your curiosity.

    —Allow yourself to be present to the voice or the image that comes through.

Notice what is awakening.

    —Be open to the unexpected.

Write this down and place the paper in the back pages of this book as a touchstone.

    —You may come back to this at different points in your journey.

The teachings and journeyings I share with you in this book have changed lives. My hope is that they will change yours for the better.

    Are you ready? Let's begin.

Part 1

Internal Discovery

Chapter 1

Following Curiosity

Each of us yearns to find our way home and reclaim our life's purpose, our destiny. Sometimes we find a well-trod path to follow, but often we must forge our own way. Yet the means exist by which we can discover the way ahead. The foundation to everything you will learn in this book begins with following your curiosity. Everyone has the capacity to follow their curiosity and to travel the inward path to the transformative power of the Imagination Matrix. This is a reflective practice, akin to meditation, yogic breathing, or other forms of contemplative exercise to which you devote daily attention and intention.

Since I was a little boy, I've been curious about my dreams. As I grew older, my curiosity extended to waking life, as if the world were a dream. What I have found over the decades is that both my professional and personal life are enhanced when I host curiosity.

Elder Turtle

I have been swimming in oceans all my life, having grown up in California. This morning, I was on a working vacation in Maui, Hawai'i. As I entered the sea, the waters were particularly warm and crystal clear. My thinking mind turned off. I watched as brightly colored tropical fish of many shapes and sizes elegantly swam along the tinted coral reefs. As my breath deepened, I became a participant, not an observer, in the orchestration of underwater wonder.

At first, I noticed a sea turtle swimming along the reef's edge. Nothing out of the ordinary, particularly in these waters. Buoyant, afloat just under the surface, he stationed himself directly in front of my scuba mask and looked me straight in the eye. I stopped swimming. I too became still, suspended in liquid space. As our engagement continued, I noticed something more. This sea turtle was big and old. His expansive brown-green shell was weathered by the salts of the sea and the growth of algae that had accumulated over the years. His eyes were huge, black-brown, set in deep sockets on both sides of his protruding head, looking both at and through me. And we recognized each other. I was with an elder. It was as if we were touching soul to soul.

When I moved ever so gently, so did he. Without turning his head away, he continued to look at me. I returned the eye contact. We remained for a moment in presence with each other. Then, with a nod of his head, he very slowly glided to a small opening in the coral, as if to invite me. I followed. Now swimming—more like drifting—as a twosome, he led me into the shelter of a small cove. Here we continued our contact, two journeyers, communicating between species in the language of elderhood. At once, his name announced itself: Elder Turtle.

Following Curiosity

As important as the senses are to the perpetuation of a safe and fulfilling life. Elder Turtle's luminous presence came to me because I followed my curiosity, which by its very nature is an invitation into deeper dimensions of awareness. Curiosity—the desire to know—is a powerful motivator for learning and shaping behavior. Research has shown that greater curiosity is associated with more creativity.[1] A recent meta-analysis across ten studies and 2,692 individuals also found "a significant association between them."[2] In addition, curiosity, interest, and surprise are key to sustaining creativity.[3] This in turn enables people to generate new or useful ideas, products, artistic expression, and a more rewarding quality of life.

Having worked with students in the university, patients in clinical practice, and employees in companies of all sizes over many years, I have found that as curiosity opens, creativity increases, and anxiety and depression decrease. Following curiosity is the key to sustaining well-being. Seeing even the familiar in a different way, you are imbued with wonder, the ultimate magic of experiencing what is new. You see the mystery of what lives below as well as the beauty displayed on the surface of things.

This happened with Ben, a premed student who came to see me because he was feeling paralyzed by anxiety. He had been told since childhood that to be successful in the world he would need to go to medical school and become a doctor. He applied himself to his studies with all that he could bring. His mode of thinking and studying narrowed in focus, driven by an intense, single-minded purpose. As the semesters went by, he became increasingly agitated and contracted. To help Ben reduce his increasingly acute levels of anxiety, I shared with him a simple way that he could reconnect with an inner state of well-being by following curiosity.

I asked Ben to slow down his usual pace when doing errands in town and instead imagine that he was a tourist visiting Santa Barbara, just taking in the sights, scents, and scenery. Afterward, he told me that he was awestruck. For the first time since he had lived here, he noticed the finely hewn Spanish-style architecture, the sound of the breeze through the palm trees, and the salty scent of the nearby ocean. Following curiosity, he experienced the magic of the place, the enchantment that he had felt long ago but had lost in the routine of his studies. Ben was so pleased that he experimented with this practice for the next several weeks in numerous locations: at the park, on the beach, in the mountains. He noticed that as he spent more time and became more interested in the natural world, his breath slowed, and he felt more spacious inside himself.

He reconnected with what had originally given him joy and purpose. He no longer felt anxiety.

When he shared all this with me, he broke into a wide smile. "I know that the life script I have been following is completely wrong for me," he declared. The next semester, Ben withdrew from the premed track. He enrolled in a program for environmental studies, where he excelled. Learning how to follow curiosity set Ben on the path to his true calling.

Burning Man

Dust storms had kicked up, coating everybody and everything with layers of sand. We moved toward the cover and shield of a tent, but we were not so lucky to be near camp. We simply sheltered in place. There is a saying among "Burners," those who frequent the annual Burning Man festival: "The playa offers a fate of its own." Burning Man, which began in 1986 as a small gathering of seekers and friends on Baker Beach in San Francisco, has now become an internationally famous two-week pop-up municipality lovingly inspired by creatives, tech giants, film-makers, and more in the remote Black Rock Desert of Nevada.

The playa is itself a place of stunning otherworldly vistas and dramatically changing light that naturally takes you from your everyday life to somewhere . . . else. At night, Black Rock City, the name given to this temporary town, becomes a festival of lights, music, and artistic activity of a thousand kinds. As people turn on the lights illuminating their camps, bikes, and bodies, another kind of light illuminates. Away from the time/space/place metrics of the known and predictable, an awakened curiosity about ourselves and others begins to take hold. The "default world" and personas we inhabit in our daily lives fade, and our authentic selves emerge. Who and what arrives at Burning Man often surprises.

One late afternoon, two friends and I had set out on our bikes, planning to follow our curiosity and engage with the wonder of all that came our way. Then, the unexpected! Which, frankly, *is* the expected at Burning Man. An unanticipated dust storm came out of nowhere with a force and density that within seconds created whiteout conditions.

Lying face down on the sandy desert floor, we waited it out, immobilized. Even contact with my friends only five feet away was impossible. And when the day turned to night, the only reflection we had consisted of what we had brought with us: our ability to embrace the moment.

Thankfully, just forty-five minutes after the squall kicked up, the winds subsided. The three of us slowly pulled ourselves up from the playa floor. We got back on our bikes and started to ride out into the night. Our lead friend took off and within moments . . . and vanished.

Completely gone. As if into another world. We didn't see him again until the next day.

There is another maxim of playa life: "Remember the core value of radical self-reliance." That night I added another core value: Follow Curiosity. In other words, notice what draws your attention and follow whatever or whoever captivates you. The playa tenders its own mysteries and shares them with you in quiet whispers and the wails of the wind: "It is time to let go of the familiar." Listen to the invisible wisdom and yield.

In the swirling wind, I allowed my Curious Mind to open. I walked ahead blindly, letting all the sensations guide me. I finally came to my Camp, HeeBeeGeeBee, one of the festival's healing areas. No one welcomed me. I was covered in dust; no one recognized me. No one even knew that I had been gone, lost. I felt the pathos of isolation. In a festive gathering of eighty-five thousand community-minded folk, emotionally open, relationally present, I felt . . . alone. I was run over by a new awareness. There I was, in the social whirl of camp, without pretense; no longer identified as the founder and chancellor of Pacifica Graduate Institute, a practitioner of Dream Tending, a program of study I created; not seen as an international lecturer and consultant. And, though fully costumed, I found myself naked. Stripped of the visible (no business cards here!), I was left to navigate the invisible on my own.

Following Curiosity, I stumbled into the healers' tent. One healer invited me into her workspace, where I sat on the floor on huge pillows, still surrounded by the omnipresent desert dust and wind. She offered a simple idea: "Breathe fully and then allow your reflections and ideas to emerge." Instead of my usual reflex to lead with my mind, I was to breathe first, think second. Breathing took on a new meaning to me then, there. In the desert, I experienced the wonder and the awe of what gets discovered when, with full breath, the imagination opens. It was particularly so this night, the one I am telling you about now.

You see, Burning Man—this festival of lights, music, and ritual—is a completely unique experience. What happens on the playa unfolds out of another impulse. Unplanned, unscheduled, unleashed experiences take on a creative life of their own. What happened to me that night was a revelation that continues to live with me to this day. Burning Man, a field of the unexpected, is a real-world manifestation of what happens when the generative potency of the Imagination Matrix is accessed. It is what I have been studying, experiencing, and teaching for years and what I now share with you. I feel privileged to have been invited to visit places—Imaginal and geographical—that opened the doors to the power of imagination.

Finding Breath, the Gateway to Awareness

As I learned on the playa, Following Curiosity begins with your breath. Upon my return to my regular work in the "default world," as Burners refer to it, I began to study the therapeutic power of breath and to use it in my programs. The purpose of breath work—as it is named in contemplative practices, psychological healing, and other modes of bodywork—is primarily to produce a reset and create the ground for regenerativity. Reconnecting to harmonious patterns of breathing changes both your mindset and your neurochemistry.

Studies have shown that the breath, when correctly observed and attended to, can become a potent means of cultivating awakened perception and opening awareness.[4] Pausing and breathing breaks through routine patterns of thinking, promoting wholeness and integration.[5] It enhances somatic presence, supports well-being, and opens airways that allow you to follow your curiosity more fluidly.[6] Developing your personal praxis of breath work is essential. Here are some methods for daily use.

Foundational Template: Relaxing into Breath

Find a location. Find a place in your home or in nature free of distractions, where you can lie on your back or sit comfortably.

Close your eyes and scan your body for tension. A simple way to scan is with your hands. Start at the top of your head. Lightly bring touch all the way down your body, through your legs to your feet. As you do so, notice where the muscles are tight. Pay particular attention to your chest and abdomen. As you notice tension in various areas, pause and breathe deeply in a way that helps you relax and release the tightness.

Move your body. When you feel stressed or upset, clenching or tightness in the jaw is a common phenomenon that constrains our breathing. Make exaggerated open-and-shut, back-and-forth motions with your mouth to release your jaw. Many find it useful to imagine that they are an actor or singer preparing to go onstage, doing warm-up exercises before a performance. Do this eight times, each time more exaggerated than the last; have fun with it. Adding sound sometimes helps the release as well and opens the throat channel for deeper breathing. Adapt this method to what works best for you.

Find focus. If you want to go a step further, gently place one hand on your throat. Bring your focus to your touch and breathe into this area. Moving your hand from throat to chest, to stomach, to legs, to feet, breathe into each area. Easy does it. Now relax your hand by your side and take three deep breaths, gently directing your breath from head to toe. There is no right way of doing this. Simply follow your body's response.

Sit in stillness. To conclude the sequence, take some time to simply be still. Let yourself relax and feel the floor or chair supporting your body. Let your busy mind relax and your Curious Mind open as you continue breathing in a natural way. Then, as you go back into the world, notice the effect that relaxing into your breath has on your body, mind, and mood. Continue to Follow Curiosity.

Staying in Presence

Most of the time, our rational mind pushes aside our capacity for curiosity. But breath opens awareness; awareness opens your experience of presence as well as a sense of wonder. Being in the world with wonderment helps you Follow Curiosity even more fully. When you are in your sense of wonder, your awareness is not narrowed down to your focused attention only.

Here's an example. The most common style of walking down the street is to move with an intent, to get to a destination as soon as possible. Moving in this way, you are operating from the rational mind in a state of laser focus, which separates you from the people, places, and activities on all sides of you. However, if you walk that same route while consciously practicing deep breathing and Following Curiosity, something altogether different unfolds. When you are in presence and curiosity, you see and hear who else is around you, and you are open to the unexpected. A building you have passed a hundred times suddenly reveals something of its unique architecture that appeals to you. A shopkeeper you have known for over ten years becomes the source of new interest, even fascination. The world comes alive. When you Follow Curiosity, an awareness arises of what exists behind and around focused rationality. As the context—not only the content—of your life shifts, you gain access to a much broader field of consciousness.

Shifting Context

Shifting Context, changing your modes of perception, is foundational to all that follows in this book. Shifting Context from the familiar to the undiscovered is elemental to entering the Imagination Matrix.

It is worth saying again: you have been trained since childhood to develop your rational modes of thinking and problem-solving. Modern culture is organized around and depends on your capacities to analyze, reason, and connect the dots. Ours is a person-centered "me" culture. The orienting questions become: *How am I feeling? What does this have to do with me?* and *How can I figure this out?* In responding to these questions, you are trained to give value to and lead with rational modes of thinking and observing.

Shifting Context allows you to move from linear thinking to spatial awareness. As you do this, something notable occurs. Your curiosity activates, and you begin to follow its lead. You sense yourself becoming a participant in the deeper realms of creativity, imagination, and soul. Here, beneath and behind the visible, exist the ever-flowing streams of psychic life sometimes referred to as qualities of the Tao.[7] Shifting Context is key to opening your Curious Mind.

Opening the Curious Mind

Finding Breath, Staying in Presence, and Shifting Context are fundamental skills. Opening your Curious Mind is always your starting point on the journey to the Imagination Matrix. Activation of your Curious Mind opens the doors of perception. It begins when you feel at ease with Shifting Contexts in an intentional way. This is not hard to do. But in a world with so many distractions, to engage in sustained reflective practice takes intention. Opening your Curious Mind brings its own rewards. When inside the experience, your body calms down, and you breathe more deeply.

The methods I teach you in this book begin with this concept and with this practice. It is when your Curious Mind is opened that the unexpected presents itself. Moving outside of egocentric experience, you can engage in the world around you in a different way. Through learning the tools and praxis, you experience a reconnection to the universal. Subsequently, you are able to discern your own uniqueness and what you are meant to contribute to the wider communities.

This occurred with Marla, who came to see me in my clinical psychotherapy practice in a state of despair. She was very depressed and, in her words, feeling "frozen." She was in her third year of a kind of life "stagnation." The medicines her doctor prescribed her helped relieve some of the "dark times," but the underlying unhappiness persisted. Marla was, as she put it, going through the motions without a sense of purpose, let alone inner joy.

When working with Marla, I added something more to the traditional treatments of psychological care, increased activity, change in diet, and new medications. In our sessions, we explored ways of opening curiosity. To start, I suggested she mark the beginning of each activity with the praxis of opening her Curious Mind. I asked her to notice what sounds she heard, what colors came forward, what feelings stirred. Following Curiosity five or six times a day for short periods had a profound and impactful effect. Marla's depressive and isolating mood began to change. Yielding to her instinctive inquisitiveness allowed Marla to tap into the life force in and around her. It is very difficult to be depressed and curious at the same time.

Foundational Template: Opening the Curious Mind

Begin your practice with a welcoming attitude. Give yourself all the time you need, without preconceived expectations, as you follow this comfortable and supportive four-step process. Be patient; the experience will take on a gentle life of its own. Find a space in which you can be undisturbed for at least ten minutes. Spend a few minutes feeling the energy come up from the earth, first into your legs, then throughout your whole body. Let this resonance from feeling grounded move through your bones. Literally feel it in your bones.

First: Deepen into your breathing and begin to shift your context. Now, with eyes closed, set your intention. Imagine being on an adventure. Notice that your skin begins to tingle as your mind enlivens. What landscape are you in; who or what do you encounter? What feelings arise—fear, joy, anxiety, excitement, sorrow, yearning?

Second: Let go of being in charge. Imagine that you are dissolving, becoming increasingly permeable and open. Take a moment and experience a release from your busy mind, what is sometimes referred to as a *state of not knowing*.

Third: In this quieter, more peaceful state of mind, take the next few minutes and imagine putting on a pair of glasses that allow you to see the beauty that lives under and on the surface of things. Notice how your body opens and your breath deepens as you imagine this more spacious way of perceiving.

Fourth: Complete the practice by extending your exploration outward. As you now prepare yourself for your day, consider how you will utilize your Curious Mind to stay in your presence with all you encounter as you go into the world.

Toward the end of his life, archetypal psychologist James Hillman, reflecting on the power of curiosity and courage, offered: "Follow curiosity, inquire into the important ideas, risk transgression. This takes courage, by which I mean letting go of old ideas, and shifting the significance of the events we fear. I mean the courage to be curious."[8] This courage to turn toward curiosity is key. As Jungian analyst Marion Woodman said to me, "Curiosity opens the way into the dance, the eternal dance of life."[9]

I ask you now to Follow Curiosity so you, too, can experience the eternal dance of life. With your Curious Mind fully open and activated, the way forward is down, through the Dig. As the poet e. e. cummings wrote: "now the ears of my ears are awake and now / the eyes of my eyes are opened."[10]

Chapter 2

Journeying in the Realms
of Deep Imagination

It began for me in one of the ubiquitous small coffeehouses in the Pacific Northwest, in the town of Everett, Washington, about ninety minutes north of Seattle. A not-very-dramatic dream had visited the night before, and I sat with my journal to do what I most often do with dreams: I wrote it down. In the dream, water was bubbling down a creek behind a shopping mall in the neighborhood where I grew up. After writing down this rather sparse description in between coffees and homemade pastry, using my barely functioning pen, I sketched the scene onto a napkin. Then, as I continued to doodle, something more opened. The creek came to life, animated by my remembrance of this actual place, a setting that I visited somewhat secretly over the years when growing up. My repeated sketches on the napkin seemed to have a magical effect. I quite literally felt the motion of flowing water from that long-ago creek.

I kept drawing. A circle appeared, getting increasingly wider and spiraling inward. I have spent a lifetime exploring underwater oceanic places, deep-water diving with a tank or free diving with snorkel and mask. In my dreams, too, I have always experienced an oceanic sensation. But here I was being invited instead to journey down below the water, into the ground underneath. Now, sitting in this coffee shop, I experienced an entryway into land-based geologic places. These were places of dirt, stone, caves, and tree roots. I had a choice to make. I hesitated. *This is ground, not ocean. How mundane*, I thought. *Not much life in this inanimate landscape.* I stopped myself, got up, paid the bill, and left the coffeehouse.

However, as if orchestrated from above—or below—that very afternoon an esteemed mentor, Russ Lockhart, encouraged me: "An opening has presented itself. Now go explore." I decided to pay attention to the call.

That evening, during one of those white nights of the Pacific Northwest, where the light dims but never really gives way to the night, I returned to the coffee shop and sat at the same table. Now, with renewed curiosity, I began the trek. I named this experience *the Geologic Dig*, not knowing then that this expedition would lead, step by step, to a realm as immense as the cosmos and as singular as my personhood itself.

My first exploration had started simply with those few doodles on the napkin that morning. I often amuse myself by sketching meaninglessly on paper. I suspect you might do the same. Yet this time, something new happened as I continued to sketch on napkin after napkin. I had the sense that the designs were emerging from a deeper place.

Over time, I allowed the process to continue to unfold. As the months and years passed since that first exploration, each Dig went a bit further. But always in a similar direction—down, vertically. Once down, I found that the geologic landscape yielded to an expanse of limitless journeying. In the beginning, in my desire to get there, I would rush. I tried to push my way to the other side. This strategy met with mixed results. Mostly with frustration and futility.

With practice, however, I discovered another way. If I became still, quiet, and uncoupled from my rational mind, my Curious Mind would open. When I allowed myself to slow down and to listen patiently, new intimations arose from the mysteries. Continuing this practice, I found that the Dig offered access to the ever-present yet unseen intelligence of psychic reality, initiating a pathway to profound insight.

The ancients and shamans knew this when they went deep into caves, climbed to remote mountaintops, and did walkabouts. Modern seekers and creatives have looked to find this awareness through plant-based inducements, meditation, or mindfulness. All of these practices have offered people much in the way of awakened consciousness. But that night in the coffeehouse, as I yielded to the designs and visions that came to me, I found another, equally rewarding approach to opening creativity, universal connection, and heightened awareness. The Dig is essentially an immersion into the Curious Mind. This praxis became foundational to the psychospiritual process of journeying in the realms of deep imagination. The Dig is the entry point of the Imagination Matrix.

The Dig

Undertaking this journey inwards is not new. Rather it is an ageless pilgrimage that is perhaps even more important today than in times past.

To deny the soul's longing is to become separate from the call, which results in stagnation and psychological paralysis. Creativity withers, and imagination dims. Researchers have found that multiple motivations drive interior reflection. Unfolding awareness, reinvention, remembrance, and insight all motivate contemplative and therapeutic inner journeying.[1]

The antidote to being disconnected from your soul's calling is to go underground. It was there that I discovered the *numinous*, Jung's word for the curiosities that the logical mind cannot explain. The idea is that the healing forces live in what Jung named the unconscious, not visible to the conscious eye, yet alive in the inner realms. The journey underground has become my own medicine.

I go on the Dig nearly every morning. It is my daily praxis. Before getting out of bed or turning to my cell phone, I take those moments between sleep time and waking time to first reflect on which dreams visited through the night. In this liminal space, a kind of time out of time, I remain receptive. Unless the imagery is very strong, I forget the visitations from the nighttime journey. The day's concerns rush in so quickly. So, first thing, I pause and write down feelings, images, or full dreams in my journal.

Then, I make a cup of tea. I move into the front room of our home and settle in a chair with a view of the trees and sky out the window. With dream figures or emotions alive in my memory, I take some time to make associations with the circumstances of my life. I ask: *Who's visiting now? What's happening here? What is the dream's desire?* I become aware that, in addition to having meaning for my life, the figures of dreams also have a life of their own. This simple reflection reawakens my curiosity and sparks my imagination. With tea in hand, journal at my side, and headphones on (I like the accompaniment of selected music), I am ready to enter the Dig. When my eyes are closed and my perception turns inward, the Imaginal lights come on. The intelligence and guidance that I bring back from the worlds behind the visible world inform my daily tasks, my writing, and my lectures, as well as my sense of destiny, my life purpose.

You will have your own experience of the Dig. You decide where and how to travel. As your Dig experience deepens, new vistas reveal themselves, along with soul figures waiting to be greeted and known. I invite you to take from this process what works for you. You might choose to do this in the same place every day, or you might choose different places, at different times. There is no one right way. Life is uncharted. As scientist and philosopher Alfred Korzybski remarked, "The map is not the territory."[2]

In the field of depth psychology, the primary point of access is emotional pain. Identifying and then transmuting suffering is a process of layering. First you locate the affliction (physical or psychological) that is creating the pathos. Then you acknowledge the personal behavior patterns (past and present) that contribute to the disharmony. Next, you amplify similar circumstances found in myth, legends, fairy tales, movies, literature, et cetera. And lastly, you find the elemental perspectives that offer insights into the wounding. Similarly, the descent into the Dig—the journey within—can take you from pain and challenge to new understandings.

Beginning and Grounding

Preparation for the Dig is quite practical. The first step is to literally find your place of departure from which to enter new realms of awareness. It is important to locate yourself in a place that is away from external demands (lists, challenges, obligations, distractions, etc.) This can be anywhere that is comfortable for you; a room at home that has a door you can close or an outside place that is away from pedestrian traffic serves this purpose well. If possible, choose a place that you can come back to time and again. When you locate your spot, make sure you remove anything that hints at the rational mind and daily routine.

Start your Dig by Shifting Context. Move your attention away from outside concerns and into the movements of your Curious Mind. Allow yourself to ground. You are setting up your base camp. This is where you depart from and where you return to. It is the axis point between the above world of the everyday and the below world of deep imagination.

In the beginning, it is vital that you come prepared for your journey. Your Dig experience requires certain tools. Assemble paper for writing and sketching or a device that allows you the capacity to write and doodle. Remember, separation from the demands or the news of the day is important. As you would in preparing for any journey, identify the resources, navigational tools, and persons you would need to make travel optimal. Think both literally and imaginatively when preparing to explore the inner realms.

For example, Claudia brought to her Dig her laptop computer, some art supplies, and some significant figures that continue to be active in her Imaginal life. Present were the remembrance of her mentor, a person who offered her intellectual and creative guidance through many years. She also brought a picture from childhood of her dog, a deeply felt protector, playmate, and beloved. Animals are particularly good companions when going on a Dig. Their instinctual intelligence is very helpful in guiding the way. In addition, Claudia brought a recurring figure from her dreams. This entity was somewhat menacing, but, as you will learn, often nightmarish images when Transmuted have the capabilities you will need in initiating and sustaining your journey.

Foundational Template: The Descent

Take a moment and imagine journeying into another dimension of consciousness. Close your eyes and bring your awareness inside, away from outer distractions. Reflect. Is there a place or landscape that evokes your curiosity? Now, in your imagination, return to this place. Follow Curiosity. Take your time here. What is the temperature of the air on your skin? What scents do you smell? Continue exploring. Let whatever is here find you. Notice who or what greets you. Offer greetings and continue your process of discovery. Now, look about. Find a place, like a cave, structure, tree, or creek, that invites you over. Pause. Look closely. How might this be a portal into another realm, a world behind the world? Prepare to make entrance in the ways that are available to you. With these beings, supplies, and tools, you are ready to embark on your descent.

Center yourself. Bring awareness to your breathing. Inhale for just a few moments, then exhale; repeat. Take a few minutes to slow down. Disengage from the external world and come inside—to yourself.

Root deeper. Imagine that you have roots extending down from your body connecting you to the earth.

Find your personal rhythm. Now that you have some separation from the demands of the external world, pause and find your presence, your personal rhythm. Notice how your body is feeling—more open, relaxed? Before moving on, Follow Curiosity: let a new sense of wonder open your Curious Mind.

Identify a supportive presence. Allow the image of a supportive presence to come into your awareness. This may be a trusted friend, an elder, a mentor, a wise teacher, or a family member, such as an unconditionally supportive grandparent, aunt, or uncle. It might even be a protective tree or animal.

Find your portal. Remember a literal landscape or an Imaginal location that provided sanctuary in the past. This may be a place familiar to you either from adult life or from your childhood. Or you might imagine it to be a cave, or a primordial opening in the earth, or a dark cellar. This memorable place will serve as your gateway into the inner worlds. Once identified, put a marker here.

Open the portal. Now you are ready to enter into a place of deeper consciousness; you are about to step off the straight and narrow path and onto the road less traveled. You might be filled with enthusiasm, or you may experience apprehension, even some fear. Trepidation at the beginning is normal. After all, ours is a culture of the bright lights. We are creatures of the above worlds. Even when the sun sets, we turn lights on everywhere to extend the experience of daytime. In modernity, taking time to go to the dark hidden places within comes with its challenges.

Your portal will be unique to your experience. As you enter the passageway, take a moment to become aware of your surroundings. Bring attention to how you got here, whether through memory, story, or the senses. Leave Imaginal bread crumbs to help you find your way back to this opening so you can return again and again. Breathe. Invite in a feeling of calm; trust that you can become comfortable in the unknowing. Don't be in a hurry to reach the bottom. Those attitudes are patterns from the above world and stem from the rational mind wanting to hurry up and realize the bottom line. Rather, slow down, engage in the journey itself. Follow your curiosity. What are the colors, textures, smells of this place? What captivates your attention? Before moving through the portal, take note of where you are, because this landing place is also where you make your return.

Rest in the landing place. Once you discover your landing place, allow yourself to rest and notice what you see, feel, hear, both inside and outside of yourself. Be patient; you are a newcomer. As the context shifts, the Imaginal field that you are now part of—not observing—animates and takes on a life of its own. You are no longer in Kansas; you have entered the magical, mysterious place of Oz. You will discover that this place and all who live here are as alive, in their ways, as you are. Imagine, how would it be to get to know these neighbors more fully? What might happen if you listened to their stories? What knowledge, even wisdom, is available here?

Illuminated Consciousness

You are now a participant in the realm of deep imagination, whose luminous energies are in perpetual motion. Depth psychology identifies this realm as the autonomous psyche or soul, inhabited by a multitude of psychic figures. Whatever the name or the conceptual overlay, the underlying principle is that in this dimension of consciousness, the invisibles of psychic reality exist and offer valuable perspectives and teachings. How can you receive, hear, and integrate what this other reality has to show you?

The sounds and feelings of the messages around you will be understated at first. You might hear a quiet voice or feel a soft presence. Allow yourself to become more receptive. Let the stories come to life. Welcome them. Don't question or try to make immediate rational sense of them. Your presence here means that your initiation into another way of seeing, listening, and being has reached an evolved stage. This is the state of *Illuminated Consciousness*. It is a quality of awareness in which you see and feel the Imaginal presence in all beings. The beauty and wonder alive in the people, creatures, places, and things of the world shine more brightly. Life takes on additional breadth and meaning. A resonant quality begins to pulse through you. Your Curious Mind opens wider.

As your engagements within the Dig evolve, you will discover that the figures and landscapes you encounter have a life of their own. They are, in fact, alive with Imaginal presence, body, and pulse. You will find yourself participating as one of the many in a transpersonal field of luminosity. Everything around you becomes imbued with a quality of light and motion. You experience your personal afflictions, yearnings, and memories within a bigger context. Figures from archetypal narratives, mythologies, and literature, like the hero/heroine, the warrior, the muse, or the magician, might appear. Listen, experience, see, feel, open yourself up to this realm. It now becomes possible to bring this Illuminated Consciousness back with you to help you face the challenges of the everyday world with new vibrancy.

Foundational Template: The Return

The signal to return presents itself differently at different times and in varying circumstances. You may simply feel the urge from within to begin the voyage back. Or one of the figures you have interacted with may offer a gesture indicating it is time to journey back to the above world. On occasion, the impulse is more practical. The demands of the day require your attention. The following simple techniques invite the profound.

Follow the one word. Use the bread crumbs you left along the way to guide you back up to the portal you stepped through to initiate your journey. Your ascent will likely be faster than on the way down. The more familiar you become with this corridor, the more confident you will be in traversing it.

Pause. Before you make your final emergence into the upper world of consciousness and life circumstances, pause. It is important to keep your experience of living between two worlds alive.

Remember. Now that you're back above, hone in on one or two teachings or experiences that you unearthed in the worlds below.

Imagine. Allow yourself to visualize simple, doable ways that you can act on behalf of your new discoveries in your daily life.

Offer gratitude. Offer your kind thoughts to those you met below and to yourself for orchestrating the time and space to Follow Curiosity.

I have found that the excursions below allow us to meet the challenges of the above world with enhanced capacities. Remarkable shifts are likely to occur in the days and months ahead in your praxis of the Dig. When you feel more grounded in the places below, you will feel increasingly grounded in your life above. Notice how you experience this altered consciousness: for some it will feel significant; for others, more subtle. You will approach your relationships and the circumstances of your life with a new perspective and renewed energetic flow.

Zuma Beach

Like many people who spend their early years living primarily in imagination, I was a sensitive, even shy, child. While Imaginal Play came easily to me, interacting with others presented many challenges. But once I entered the later grades of elementary school, becoming socially capable was not only expected, it was mandatory. In addition, the very first micro-hints of my interest in girls were beginning to reveal themselves. My imagination, so active on the inside, had yet to come outside, let alone be shared with anyone else.

One day, after school, it happened. Imagination presented itself at the tide pools on Zuma Beach, just north of Los Angeles. A rock jetty extended into the sea and separated the beaches north and south. The north beach was supervised and civilized, a public beach popular with families. The south beach was a mystery. The accepted rules of order stipulated that no curious kid should ever venture there. *Why are we not allowed there?* My curiosity got the best of me.

When the tide was at its lowest, one could simply walk over the exposed jetty to the south. I did so and jumped down onto the sand. I looked all around me, taking it all in. Glistening tide pools appeared in every direction; the receding waves had exposed long lines of brightly colored, iridescent coral; and hundreds of sea anemones and starfish, still trembling with life, dotted the beach.

Sitting down on a piece of sea-worn coral, I watched and listened to the teeming activity in this majestic corner of nature. Mesmerized, I was suspended in time, but was startled to attention by a voice behind me. *What am I hearing?* I wondered. *What voice is whispering in my ear?* The words were subtle, yet direct. My attention was captivated.

"Did you know that rocks can talk?" The words were haunting and prophetic. I was speechless. Who was speaking, and how did he know? I did not think that anybody other than me could hear such things! I turned around to see a surfer in his late teens, a god of the highest order to a twelve-year-old. He smiled at me and walked down the beach. I was transformed by his words, which affirmed my secret sense of the world around me. *I wasn't alone. Other people could experience the animated voices of nature.* With this affirmation, they became stronger, more expressive, and my hearing grew sharper.

Eventually, I was jolted from my reverie by an earthly reality: the tide was coming in! I hopped off the reef and landed safely on the supervised beach once again, where my parents awaited.

"Steve, where have you been?" my mother asked. For me, this was an all-too-familiar question!

What could I say? *I have been betwixt and between worlds to a place where gods exist, where rocks can talk, and where the landscape has stories to tell. I have just witnessed the place where my fate awaits.* No. Here on the well-traveled side, where food stands, parking lots, and lifeguards secured the beachscape, rocks did not speak, the ocean and her creatures remained mute, and the destination was always of a future many thousands of miles down the road of life.

Now, looking back, I see that what was revealed to me that day, after school, at the ocean, was my first conscious awareness of another destination, my destiny, making a call.

Destiny

Your destiny is found on the other side, the Imaginal side, which is always present, forever waiting to be known once you learn how to access it. Like my experience on Zuma Beach or your journey into the realms of deep imagination in the Dig, your fate reveals itself when you have the courage to open your Curious Mind and let yourself go off script. As Joseph Campbell said: "Don't be afraid, doors will open where you didn't know they were going to be. If you follow your bliss, doors will open for *you* that wouldn't have opened for anyone else."[3]

Chapter 3

Soul Companions

When you travel to new places, it is helpful to have guides who facilitate your experience, much as sherpas do on mountain climbs. This also applies to traveling the internal route to deep imagination. As you journey more frequently along the pathways of the Dig, your Curious Mind opens. You will notice that such helpful figures begin to appear. These figures are your *Soul Companions*. They will be your guides, protectors, and teachers as you navigate the Imagination Matrix.

While this concept might at first seem odd, throughout human experience figures of imagination have shaped who we are and who we become. My own fieldwork verifies one overarching finding: Imaginal figures, Soul Companions, are elemental psychoactive forms influencing the behavior and emotions of a person's life. Qualitative research in the field of depth psychology shows that these figures of imagination have primacy, and they impact and influence our behavior. This insight provides the critical foundation for my theories regarding the importance of Soul Companions in the work of exploring the Imagination Matrix.

Soul Companions can present themselves as persons, animals, landscapes, and mythic presences. Some might already be known to you. As you get to know and trust these allies on your journey in the realms of deep imagination (below), you will find often in surprising ways that they also become Imaginal allies you can draw upon in daily life (above). When developing this relationship, Soul Companions assist you in meeting psychological, emotional, and physical challenges.

A classic example of this is found in *The Wizard of Oz*, when those figures Dorothy knew in her life on the Kansas farm became the Scarecrow, Lion, Tin Man, Wizard, and Witches of the East and West in the realm of Oz. Each possessed attributes that proved to be useful on her journey along the yellow brick road and even more so coming home to her own backyard.

Landscapes as Soul Companions can also have a significant role to play. They come with a sense of presence and place. A temenos is a sacred place or landscape. In the waking world, it most often refers to a piece of ground surrounding or adjacent to a temple or a revered sanctuary. Familiar examples of temene are the historic Parthenon in Greece, England's Stonehenge, Göbekli Tepe in Turkey, and South Dakota's Black Hills. Nature places that hold hallowed significance for a community, like springs, river crossings, groves of trees, oceanscapes, desert vistas, and venerated mountains also carry the soulful resonance of temene. Think of the spirits in the trees of an enchanted forest or the muses waiting at Mount Shasta, California.

Examples of animal or nonhuman guides as Soul Companions are many. Animal figures from Western stories, such as the *Alice in Wonderland's* White Rabbit and *Oz's* Toto, take on leadership qualities and guide the way into the unfamiliar aspects of the Imagination Matrix. In Native traditions, Coyote, Dog, Goanna, and Eagle emerge as animal spirits leading the way through vision quests and walkabouts. Beloved pets from throughout your life may also become Soul Companions when remembered as participants in the journeys through the Imagination Matrix.

The stories told through your Soul Companions offer timeless insight and knowledge. They are the stuff of myth, fairy tale, and legend and the keys to the collective knowledge of human experience. I have found, through personal experience, that cultivating relationships with my Soul Companions offers insight and teachings related to the circumstances of my life as well as opening the way to the boundless mysteries of existence.

Odysseus and His Soul Companions

Perhaps one of the best descriptions of the presence and influence of Soul Companions is in the epic poem of ancient Greece *The Odyssey*. It is the story of the struggles and triumphs of the hero, Odysseus, as he makes his way home to Ithaca after the Trojan War. In the telling, we hear and learn about the profound impact Soul Companions have on a person's life journey.

The Odyssey begins with Odysseus, king of Ithaca, still not returned home from war because he angered Poseidon, the god of the sea. Odysseus's protectress, the goddess Athena, asks Zeus, king of the gods, to allow Odysseus to return home. Athena assists Odysseus with divine powers throughout the epic journey, and she speaks up for him in the councils of the gods on Mount Olympus. She often appears in disguise as a mentor. Without this supportive Soul Companion, his return home would have been impossible.

Odysseus's journey is also filled with many obstacles and oppo-sitional figures. He is betrayed and hindered by foes, including the Sirens and the Cyclops. In his adverse encounters with them, he finds assistance from his Soul Companions on his journey back to Ithaca.

My Soul Companions

Over the course of many years, I have gathered my own cohort of Soul Companions who counsel and guide me. I meet them daily in my Dig practice, which I always begin in my home space, settled in a comfort-able seat, with facilitative music turned on. I deepen into my breath, come into presence, and open my Curious Mind. I offer an invitation that I say out loud: "The CALL goes out, the GATHERING begins."

I encounter otherworldly Imaginal landscapes, each offering a ground of knowledge that informs my above-world life. The inhabitants of these hallowed places tell stories of their own making, not simply projections of my construction.

Many figures assemble, but I wait for the three particular Soul Companions who always accompany me further and deeper. They are GUIDE, who leads the way; an animal presence called CATT; and BELOVED, who offers both support and protection. Once gathered, we are ready. GUIDE and/or CATT provides the gesture to commence. We follow.

✤ Foundational Template: Receiving Teachings from Soul Companions

The wisdom gleaned from the persons, animals, and landscapes that you encounter in the realms of deep imagination constitutes a learning of the highest order. Lead with your curiosity and presence. Learning comes from listening deeply before reacting and sustaining your curiosity before getting analytical. Slow down and experience receiving before pushing for answers to any questions you might have. Remember, you are a guest, a newcomer to these realms, being hosted in new places by unique communities. Be patient. Experience the welcome; breathe. Follow the lead of your Soul Companions and the others who are with you. Allow yourself to receive the teachings being offered.

Begin with the Dig. Ground yourself in your Imaginal place. Start your Dig practice, journeying down through the now-familiar layers, and come to a landing place.

Become a naturalist. Observe the activities in as much detail as you can, much as a naturalist would in a new setting. Under your patient observation, the persons and places of this realm will become more animate.

Notice the particularity of what/who is being witnessed. As persons, places, and things become increasingly visible and distinct, note their sizes, colors, shapes, markings, and other details.

Use your senses. Experience each Soul Companion as an embodied Imaginal presence. As possible, use all your senses (sight, touch, taste, smell, listening, even curiosity) to follow their activities. Again, notice how the figures take on a life of their own.

Enter into mutual regard. With an attitude of respectful mutual regard, look into the essential quality of these living presences. Experience your breath as well as the breath of those who are journeying with you. Discover the correspondence between your body and the embodied presence of the others.

Pause. Allow yourself to feel how you are being moved by the life force flowing between the embodied figures and your body.

Attend. Receive the stories being told. Bring a witnessing presence to what is unfolding. Take field notes. Write or sketch what you are seeing and hearing. The teachings come to life in the stories. Collect what is being taught.

Who Are the Soul Companions?

There are as many inner figures as can be imagined. They can come in the form of Imaginal persons or presences, such as the Guide, the Shapeshifter, the Beloved, the Monster in the Machine, the Inner Physician, the Storyteller, Earth Mother, the Sage. Stories and myths from all cultures bring with them vast casts of characters that include Imaginal beings of every kind, an array of landscapes, and constructions both familiar and never before seen. These inner figures—some of which you will encounter in your journeys—fall into two overarching categories: supportive and shadow. They show up bringing innate gifts and occasioning emotional pathos. These figures influence emotions, actions, and sensations throughout your life. They make a claim on your body and spirit. As you develop the capacity and the willingness to receive them, you will find the special abilities these Soul Companions offer to be life changing.

Later in this chapter I will introduce you to nine major figures you are likely to meet, both supportive and shadow. We will explore other figures in the following chapters. (If you want to read further about Imaginal figures, please review the Recommended Reading at the end of the book.) First, however, I will share how to utilize their powers through two processes: Illumination and Transmutation. You can *amplify* the supportive figure's abilities through the process of *Illumination*. You will *mitigate* the shadow figure's destructive abilities, when possible, and transform them for constructive use through the process of *Transmutation*. Gathering the energies of these Soul Companions enables you to bring a new perspective and confidence from the below world to your daily experiences in work, play, and love.

Identifying Supportive Figures

In depth psychology, work has focused on the shadow, which holds those experiences people find menacing. This is because there is a belief that the shadow experience is at the root of our psychopathology. However, over the decades, I have also found it is equally beneficial to invite into consideration the Supportive Soul Companions. Though somewhat marginalized in today's world, they too are of enormous consequence.

With the overemphasis on the shadow figures—the villains and bad characters—who dominate our news and other cultural references, it seems that supportive figures have been increasingly sidelined. Friendly guides, allies, mentors, and inner figures have become almost alien. Ironically, these deeply supportive, often loving entities are turning into the shadow figures of our times. It is harder to manifest kindness, trust, and care when fear and dread, grief and tragedy dominate the culture around us.

Humans need more compassion and support in our lives now. Children often feel threatened, even afraid to go to school because of mass shooters. The newer generations of heroic action figures, their ubiquitous presence everywhere—in games, social media, and toys— are examples of this pervasive assault. In order to nurture healthy individuals, it is imperative to fully rediscover and recover the supportive figures that are being sidelined in our culture. We need the balance. I believe that this is an urgent part of psychological work for the modern day.

The Process of Illumination

When we activate supportive Soul Companions, they *Illuminate*, meaning that they come to life in the realms of deep imagination. Illumination is a process by which we recognize that living images of deep imagination have a body and pulse of their own making. Supportive Soul Companions, when Illuminated, have their own autonomous nature. They present themselves to your imagination as independent figures. Their development is separate from yours. They follow their unique paths and purposes, outside of your rational mind's control or authority. You cannot anticipate or predict their development. Yet as they evolve, you become connected into the realization of your own life's journey.

When named, then embraced, the supportive figures become guiding presences in your life. And when Illuminated, these supportive figures are essential for expanding your joy, and your sense of connection, purpose, and well-being. The presence of an Illuminated supportive figure offers the resources you need to heal. These figures can come forward in the guise of the Beloved, the Witness, the Mentor, the Shapeshifter, the Guardian, and more. For example, in the movie *Field of Dreams*, supportive figures appear by way of visions and voices: "If you build it, they will come." They often show up for children as guides. You may have experienced this in your own childhood.

In the Imaginal realms, Supportive Soul Companions often come forward with a resemblance to a truly helpful person whom you are familiar with, like a best friend, mentor, or unconditionally loving parental figure. These supportive people, or sometimes animals or places, can be either alive or dead in the above world. However, when these figures of soul become Illuminated, they gain a life of their own. They exist in the worlds below the literal world. When you invest time and energy in Illuminating their Imaginal presence, their own autonomy and activity expand. As archetypal psychologist James Hillman described, they engage in the activity of "soul-making."[1] By "setting the table" and greeting their visitation, you bring a regard and an open, Curious Mind to their presence. As your relationship intensifies, you get to know their essential being and their becoming.

The process of Illuminating Supportive Soul Companions is a way of welcoming their arrival and what I, and others, call befriending. The vital first step to befriending is seeing and experiencing your Supportive Soul Companions in their distinctive autonomy and activity. First, you recognize a companion as a familiar person, place, or animal. Then, as you open your Curious Mind, you come to know the invisible essence that is inside the literal. You begin to interact with this entity. In doing so, you evolve a relationship with the embodied presence of the one that has captured your curiosity. You begin to see, hear, and experience the wisdom, comfort, and knowledge that this figure is here to confer. When you engage in the process of listening attentively, bringing your care to the figure, the Soul Companion will, in turn, bring its care, even love, to you.

Foundational Template: Illuminating Your Supportive Soul Companions

The process of befriending Illuminates the Soul Companion. It lights the energetic field surrounding both of you. This Illuminated presence can move with you and protect you through all your internal journeys and back to the above world.

Whether you are dealing with above-world entities or below-world allies, the process of Illumination follows this sequence:

Identify. Scan both the circumstances of your awake life and the memories from your life history. Who or what comes forward as a supportive presence? Who is/was a best friend, mentor, or guardian spirit? What place or landscape holds for you a sense of deep belonging? Then, identify the supportive Imaginal figures in your dreams and imagination.

Name. Take a moment to focus on whomever or whatever has made a request for your attention. Really see into this person, animal, or landscape. Pause and reflect. Make a list of the supportive or caring attributes coming forward now. What special supportive or protective qualities do you recognize? Take note of the literal name, such as Aunt Margaret of awake life, Grandfather Raúl, who has passed. Do the same for dream images, like that of your childhood pet dog Kia. Next, notice if a deeper name lives behind the surface. It may be a single word modifier, like Wise Grandfather Raúl or Beloved Kia. Don't forget supportive landscapes. The grove of trees or quiet city street that you spend time in when seeking sanctuary might be named Sacred Grove.

Illuminate. Now, Shift Context, as on your Dig; perceive through a new lens. Bring a witnessing presence to the supportive figure. Breathe, open your Curious Mind, and see with an Imaginal eye. Notice how the person, place, or animal comes to life in a new way. Stay with this process. Be patient. Allow the figure, in its autonomy, to come forward and enliven. Notice how the figure gains an embodied presence of its own. Take the time to witness the becoming. The process of Illumination continues as you give expression to who and what is visiting now. As the figure or landscape deepens in its revealing, give description to what you are witnessing: sketch, sculpt, doodle, and/or move to what is emerging. You are greeting, then befriending, your supportive Illuminated Soul Companions in an ongoing process. Their evolution invites your own.

Offer gratitude. Now that your Illuminated Supportive Soul Companions are present, tender gratitude to the Illuminated inner community. It is helpful to do so at the beginning and at the end of each journey.

When Supportive Soul Companions are Illuminated, they are no longer part of somebody else's psychological or theological explanatory system; their predetermined purpose is gone. Through your witnessing presence, you give expression to the Supportive Soul Companions' Illuminated presence. These companions come into their innate spontaneity and generativity. Their psychic life force awakens. Listen attentively, bring your care, and give your regard to the figures. Allow yourself to experience the wisdom, comfort, and knowledge they have come to offer you.

An example of this Illumination process happened with one of my clients. Jessica was in a difficult place in her life when she came to see me. The negative self-talk that began in her childhood was holding her back from taking steps to meet others. Both of Jessica's parents were critical by nature. Jessica felt alone, unseen, and unsupported. The one person who was there for her was her Aunt Marna, who was caring and encouraged Jessica's artistic talent.

By attending my workshops, Jessica learned how to open her Curious Mind and engage with her Soul Companions. Many were people she recognized from the above world—her career mentor, her childhood pet, and, most happily, her beloved Aunt Marna, who had passed over and was now alive as a memory. Jessica followed the Illumination steps, deepening her relationship with her aunt in the Imaginal here and now. Through this process, Jessica experienced something different. Not only did Aunt Marna offer support, but that support now Illuminated into unconditional love.

Aunt Marna moved from a caring childhood presence to an unwavering champion of the adult Jessica. Jessica noticed that this Illumination expanded over time. The more she befriended her aunt in Imaginal life, the more Aunt Marna cared for her in return. Moreover, Jessica's other

Supportive Soul Companions did the same. The company and care of these companions were now present with Jessica both on her internal journeys and in her navigation of waking life circumstances. In time Jessica was able to silence the negative thoughts that had kept her in isolation. She was finally able to reach out to new people, build meaningful relationships, and live vibrantly as the artist she truly was.

The Supportive Soul Companions

The Beloved: Dearest Friend (Support, Care, Love)

The figure of the Beloved is central to all human experience. As a Soul Companion, the Beloved's presence comes forward in the personhood of a best friend, a supportive parental figure, an unconditionally loving grandparent, your child, your lover, or others. Psychologically, the Beloved's primacy in your life cannot be overstated. When self-love is present, you expand your capacities for compassion and self-care. When absent, you feel lost, even abandoned. The Beloved is a primary support figure. When you are separated from the Beloved, you can feel uncertainty, even a sense of insecurity. Deepening your relationship with the Beloved is foundational. When you have your Beloved by your side, you are ready to move forward.

The Beloved Illuminated

When Illuminated, the Beloved becomes your touchstone in both the world above and the Imaginal worlds below. The Beloved offers more than support and care: it offers unconditional love. This is a love that you feel as a deep compassion and a homecoming. When the Beloved is present, your breath deepens and your heart opens. Not only is your body affected, but also the Imaginal bodies of your many Soul Companions come to life and together surround you with care and high regard.

The Witness: Presence (Viewer, Seer, Observer)

In the above world, the role of the Witness is to provide information. Most familiar is the function of a Witness in a legal context. The eyewitness to a scene of a crime tells of what they have seen, heard, or experienced. However, being a Witness to a deeply meaningful spiritual event or ritual is also a well-known practice worldwide. In Hindu philosophy, "witness" may refer to a state of consciousness, *sakshi*. In this quality of awareness, a person experiences or sees the world but is not affected or involved. In yoga praxis, to be in a state of sakshi, to witness, is the ability to notice your thoughts without identifying with or reacting to them.[2]

A witness may simply take the time to observe, as someone who summons their patience and presence to see all that is around them with an aesthetic eye, appreciating the details of a landscape or circumstance.

The Witness Illuminated

When Illuminated, the Witness provides a quality of deep presence and attuned awareness. Crucial for gathering information, the Illuminated Witness lovingly sees and reflects all that you are here to discover and all that you are becoming. Often, it is an animal figure—like Wise Owl, Intelligent Wolf, Observant Dolphin, Seeing Dog, or Independent Cat—that is especially vested with keen instinct and attuned sense to perceive the radiance that exists at the center of all things. When with your Illuminated Witness, you walk the path with an engaged observer. You navigate the terrain with an accomplished tracker. You move easily around obstacles to discern what is essential. As a beholder of what simply is, without distraction, you see newly unveiled opportunities with heightened clarity. Supported by the confidence that you are protected from all that is seen and unseen, you are able to take action to fulfill your boldest dreams.

The Mentor: Wise Elder (Teacher, Guide, Counselor/Advisor)

A Mentor is a wise person who imparts advice. Your relationship with your Mentor is grounded in trust. It can be a teacher, a counselor, a parent, a friend, or others. Mentors play an essential role in guiding you through the course of your life. When you review your life, who has served in this role? Perhaps a guidance counselor at a school, a family member who offers wise advice without judgment, or a financial advisor whose expertise has earned your trust. Loyal friends assume this role, particularly in times of life transition. In all cases, the attributes of trust, wisdom, expertise, and life experience are foundational to providing the guidance you seek. Their capacity to care deeply is palpable. You will recognize these caring figures in the below world.

The Mentor Illuminated

When Illuminated, the Mentor reveals considerable knowledge and deep caring. The Mentor offers great insights and introduction to the never-before seen. An example is Morpheus in *The Matrix*, who teaches Neo the ways of the Matrix. In offering guidance, the Illuminated Mentor points you toward your calling. Illuminated mentorship is a process of perceiving the seemingly invisible path of your becoming. On your journey, with the Mentor's support and wise counsel, you forever evolve into your destiny, if you have the courage to grasp hold of it. Supported by your Mentor, you are ready to embrace what emerges.

The Shapeshifter (Changemaker, Metamorph, Chameleon, Transformer)

In cultures real and virtual, Shapeshifters exhibit abilities to adjust quickly, modify behavior on the spot, and efficiently alter their personality and appearance as the situation demands. When events turn problematic, the Shapeshifter manifests negative aspects, like manipulation, cleverness, and forgery. In extreme circumstances, they manifest afflictions like multiple identity disorder. However, more often, the attributes of shape-shifting and the person who is identified as a Shapeshifter play a generative role in both daily life and imagination.

In fantasy and mythology, a Shapeshifter can change from a human body into that of an animal. Familiar shape-shifting creatures in folklore are werewolves and serpents. Stories of their transformative capabilities are found in European, Canadian, South Asian, First Nations, and other Indigenous cultures. For example, Raven is often seen as a magical creature able to take the form of human, animal, and even inanimate objects.[3] Perhaps the most recognized Shapeshifter in Western mythology is Proteus, who could become whatever shape he pleased. One meaning of the word *protean* is "changeable in shape and form." The Shapeshifter is also present in movies and other popular forms of storytelling. Superheroes like Superman or Wonder Woman change almost instantaneously when they need to activate superpowers for doing good.

When you reflect on the supportive Shapeshifters whom you have encountered in life, think of people both living and dead. As you consider this figure more carefully, notice how through deep empathy they gain access to the genius of invention. They can mimic, but also they can invent, changing themselves or a situation from one form into another.

The Shapeshifter Illuminated

The chameleon-like aptitudes of the Shapeshifter become more amplified when Illuminated. Traversing time and space, the Shapeshifter offers access to the past and future existing in the immediacy of the present. Who better to send on an advanced mission than the Shapeshifter? With mercurial abilities to blend in and adapt to new environments, the Illuminated Shapeshifter possesses the abilities to morph into different persons, animals, even places, and to provide the means to travel between space and time. An example of an Illuminated Shapeshifter, the fictional character of Marvel's Doctor Strange serves as a sorcerer supreme, using his generative powers to protect Earth. The Illuminated Shapeshifter assimilates effortlessly into alien settings. Their capacity to shape-shift back into their original form offers you their increased empathy and knowledge. When you access the capacities of the Illuminated Shapeshifter, you see the multiplicity of the Imagination Matrix in all its infinite beauty. You feel energized by all the possibilities open to you.

The Guardian: Protector (Defender, Keeper, Watcher)

The Guardian watches over those in their care. Guardians offer protection when you are facing challenging situations or threatening life circumstances. A Guardian holds a safe container as you deal with the intensity of a life challenge. As a Soul Companion, the Guardian provides the safety needed for the care of the soul. In addition to showing up as persons, Guardians appear in animal form—often as Lion or Bear. As Guardian spirits, they defend and protect through their instinctive animal wisdom. Rituals of dance and song are often used to Illuminate their presence. Guardian figures appear with an attitude of vigilance and watchfulness.

The Guardian Illuminated

Illuminated, the Guardian gains capabilities beyond what we know in awake life. The Guardian is a watcher with eyes that can see in the dark and a protector whose superpowers ensure safe access. The Illuminated Guardian walks alongside us; their resonant field, or aura, offers safety and security. When the Guardian Illuminates, this presence may appear as a deity or a spirit, resembling either an animal or a person. In angelic presence, the Guardian becomes oracular, with abilities to perceive threat before it occurs and guard against taking the wrong turn and going off path. As a keeper of dreams and spiritual medicine, the Illuminated Guardian keeps you secure as you walk the path toward your purpose.

The Shadow Soul Companions

In depth psychology, the oppositional or perhaps seemingly devious companions are called *shadow figures*. Shadow Soul Companions are central to leading a balanced and psychologically healthy life. According to Jung, "The shadow exists as part of the unconscious mind and is composed of repressed ideas, weaknesses, desires, instincts, and shortcomings."[4] He went on to note that knowing your own darkness is the best method for dealing with the darknesses of other people. A core teaching in many wisdom traditions is that engaging and then transmuting the often split-off or repressed negative energies of the shadow figures lying in wait is the first step in deepening relationships with yourself and others.

As you extend your Curious Mind, you will notice that familiar, at times oppositional, Shadow Soul Companions appear. These figures can come forward in the guise of the Dragon, the Zombie, the Vampire, the Savior/Rescuer, and more. We all encounter Shadow figures in our journey of life. But just as with Soul Companions that seem friendly, we must continue to keep our minds open to the wisdom and teachings of the Shadow.

Shadow figures carry traits and behaviors that are generally considered unacceptable not only to society but also to our own personal values. These traits or behaviors may include envy, greed, prejudice, hate, or aggression and may result in feelings of being persecuted, victimized, or criticized. In situations of trauma, genocide, severe anxiety, or fear, I suggest that you take this process slowly so as not to trigger these wounds. A professional can be of help here. The work of Transmuting the shadow image takes mindful care. As you read through the process of Transmutation, it is important for you to modify to your own sensibilities or, when needed, to seek professional assistance. Sometimes, it is best to disidentify and witness what is arising without trying to transmute and integrate it.

The goal of inviting the Shadow Soul Companions into your journey is to discover their other side, their generative capacities. These proactive qualities are often of great use when journeying in the Imagination Matrix.

Put simply, most figures have, at core, dual characteristics. In the solar daylight of awake experience, they function in one manner, and in the lunar night-light of Imaginal experience, they may operate in a much different way. They hold the potential of bringing forth special abilities you need for the deepening and widening of your Imaginal journey. This double-sided aspect is what I call *imago duplex*. Many cultures push away, ignore, or exorcise these problematic figures and relegate the behaviors they engender to the margins. To do so we use culturally esteemed practices—psychologizing, medicalizing, and/or distracting. Of course, in some situations this is needed. However, while we believe that this makes us safe from their threatening behavior, it also means we can't access their generative powers, their potency.

An example is Luke Skywalker's Transmutation of Darth Vader in *Star Wars*. Vader was lord of death and destruction for Luke in the external world. When Luke removed Vader's mask—transmuting the Shadow figure into a Guardian and Mentor—Luke's supportive father emerges. Vader's presence, once Transmuted from an archenemy into an ally, became crucial to Luke's inner life and forward journeying. In the battles and explorations ahead, Luke would need to use Vader's teachings and powers, now part of Luke's inner resources.

What had been destructive in the above world Transmuted into valuable special abilities in the world below. But Shadow experiences do not have to be personified as figures only. The dark side of the Force, like a dark mood, is just as much a shadow for Luke as Darth Vader.

Shadow entities are frequently aspects of what your conscious mind refuses to acknowledge; you most often experience them as negative. However, paradoxically, it is in the wound that you can find what you need for the healing. Given that your psychological or personal shadow is composed of qualities, impulses, emotions, and experiences that you do not want others to see, you will tend to cast these traits into the hidden domain and/or project them onto other people.

Jung described shadow work as necessary to undertake for the process of individuation, your personal psychological development.[5]

To evolve your sense of full capability, it is important to go into the underworld of your consciousness. First, make visible, and then—with the support of allied figures—encounter, Transmute, even befriend the shadow figures. In doing so, you develop some of the most important Soul Companions—personified as figures, feelings, and landscapes—that will support and guide you.

Identifying Shadow Figures

Discovering the shadow figures that threaten your well-being is of primary importance. When they show up, you can ward off an attack before it begins; you can then neutralize and Transmute their powers. In attending to shadow figures you might see their characteristics operating in yourself or in someone near to you. As you learn the craft of Transmuting shadow figures from foes to friends to allies, the behaviors that were once destructive become generative. This can be a constructively insightful experience.

Your first step is to learn how to identify the shadow figures that personify destructive shadow experiences in your life; then, with support and protection, you work to change their energies for constructive use.

Working with shadow figures found in your everyday world offers tangible benefits in helping you enjoy a healthier, more abundant and creative life. You drain a good deal of your personal life force when, as an understandable mode of coping with shadow figures, you employ avoidance strategies or stay in isolation, given the intense power they hold and the enormous energy you invest in protecting yourself from them. It is also helpful to proactively identify shadow figures before they blindly take you over. Notice when you encounter an aggressive colleague, an unruly family member, or a neighborhood bully. With practice, when they assert their oppositional nature, instead of becoming reactive you can take a pause. First is to create some distance, get grounded, then identify the shadow figure behind the behavior. From here, you then can become proactive.

Remember, your corresponding inner Imaginal figure is not at all afraid of the oppositional traits that you encounter. As you befriend the conflictual Shadow Soul Companions within yourself, you can lean into their capabilities. They know the ways of combating fire with fire. When you are accompanied by these soul warriors, your ability to disarm the hostilities coming at you from others increases. In fact, their mere existence as your Soul Companions wards off outside attack before it gets started. It is often said that "your enemy is your best teacher."

Joanne had struggled most of her life with what she named her "Inner Critic." She suffered from childhood with the all-consuming need to be perfect in all that she did. Her relentless drive for perfection was a constant obsession. Whenever Joanne met another person with the same competitive force moving through them, fireworks erupted of the most inflammatory kind, often hostile. This occurrence was not infrequent. Often, like attracts like. After some hard work and mindful attention, Joanne came to view her Inner Critic as a figure existing outside of herself. She was able to disidentify from and evolve a relationship with this intense force. After a process of personifying this aspect of her personality, the Inner Critic became the Shadow Soul Companion "Harpy." Rather than feeling possessed by Harpy, she now felt an affiliation, even a kinship.

It did not take long to put this new companionship to work. One week following, Joanne was approached by her archrival, Marion. They had been competitors in most everything for fifteen years. What happened next was a life-changing event. Rather than getting hooked into the no-win game of one-upmanship, Joanne first turned to her Soul Companion, Harpy, and then faced Marion with Harpy by her side. Harpy was an expert player. Competition, criticism, and perfection were the stuff she was made of. With Harpy by her side as an ally, Joanne experienced the capacity to stand ground, center, and not fall into the never-ending, all-too-familiar game.

As the weeks went by and her relationship with Harpy continued to deepen, she noticed that the instances of being in competitive combat with others lessened. She simply did not attract as many of those kinds of people or situations into her life.

⊗ Foundational Template: Transmuting Your Shadow Companions

To convert the destructive shadow figures or images from the above world into below-world allies who offer constructive guidance and protection requires the process of Transmutation, which follows this sequence:

Identify. To begin, identify an emotional state that you find problematic, even at times crippling, in your life. Emotional experiences like rejection, failure, feeling left out, despair, and crippling anxiety are familiar examples. Often these oppositional emotions have been around for some years and make their grip felt over and over. Think of an experience causing you pain and through which the problematic emotion appears. Next, make a list of people you know who carry aspects of this emotion's presence. What are the ways these people exercise their power over you? What strategies or behaviors do they employ to trigger the painful reaction in you? For example, do they call you names, talk behind your back, attack or judge you on social media, use a critical facial expression?

Name. Now that you've identified this presence, its characteristics, and the strategies it uses to fuel its power over you, give it a name. How do they manipulate, con, dehumanize, torture, even kill? What "talents" do they use to torment? In both the below and the above world, these behaviors are dangerous, crippling, even life-threatening.

Transmute. Now think about how some of these negative or dysfunctional behaviors might make a positive contribution. How can the skills that were used so effectively to create great angst in your life now be used as important tools offering valuable assistance? When Transmuted into procreative forces, the nemeses of above become resourceful allies and helpful companions below.

Gratitude. When encountering conflicts in which you feel stuck, uncertain, or agitated, offer your gratitude for having the power of a Transmuted shadow figure by your side. Your Shadow Soul Companion can provide the power you need to engage and move forward.

The Shadow Soul Companions

The Dragon: Persecutor (Judge, Critic, Intimidator)

The age-old shadow figure of the Dragon embodies the tormentor. Huge in size, residing in dank caves, deep pools, wild mountain reaches, sea bottoms, and haunted forests, it is the embodiment of chaos and untamed nature. Known for its ability to judge impulsively, it strikes with a blaze of fire. With just one blast from the Dragon, you are reduced to instant death. Dragon as an intimidator is a force to be reckoned with. In its many guises, Dragon's presence is energy depleting and leads to profound insecurity, often to emotional and psychological paralysis. The Dragon represents the judgments of others or the self-critic sitting on your shoulder. Intimidation and harassment are two outcomes you experience when the Dragon is activated.

The Dragon Transmuted

After Transmutation, the Dragon becomes a Soul Companion possessing superpowers of great value. In Chinese cosmology, dragons represent noble bravery, good fortune, and power.[6] They are essential powers to ward off the tormenting inner critic and the often unbearable impact of feeling judged. Dragon brings the red/yellow fire of support and determination. This energy is the force you need to be able to explore further, to sustain engagement, and to calm down the rational mind when it activates. The fire from the Dragon creates further opportunities to Illuminate the figures of your Imaginal landscapes. You can draw from this power to counteract those who might torment or judge you in the world of daily affairs.

The Zombie: Intruder (Invader, Trespasser, Burglar)

Zombies appeared in myth and legend long before their popularity in films and TV shows. Zombies originated in Haitian folklore, but Zombie stories have shifted to meet current cultural fears and contexts.[7] They were particularly present in the nightmares of people during the 2020 COVID-19 pandemic, as I saw in my Dream Tending work with people worldwide during that time. Zombies infect bodies with deadly viruses. They are trespassers, taking over bodies of the living. One of our greatest human fears is the loss of our soul. When you feel the presence of the Zombie, you experience the threat of a burglar, intruder, trespasser; you feel invaded and hollowed out.

The Zombie Transmuted

Once Transmuted, the Zombie has many gifts, including the ability to quell the anxiety of loss and the fear of death. As a true inhabitant of the below world, this figure provides access to the teachings of the nightmarish, the intolerable, and the horrific. Who better to navigate the territory? For the Zombie this is familiar terrain. The Zombie knows that death is not dying, that death is contiguous with life at all points. The Zombie's energy, when Transmuted, can bring a visceral sense of life in the realms below. What appears at first as the world of the dead reveals itself as a world alive with substance and wonder. The Zombie Transmuted provides you with a powerful, life-affirming energy to ward off threats in a world that may feel filled with impending disaster.

The Vampire: Victimizer (Wounded, Prey, Sufferer)

The Vampire myth originated in Europe, but most cultures have tales surrounding this archetypal creature that lives by ingesting your vital essence. The blood it takes is symbolic of your life force. Drained of your vitality, you feel wounded and victimized. You become prey to danger.

When you feel this depletion—drained of your blood and beyond mortal healing—suffering and woe become constant states of being. You experience a withering of your personhood and a sense of powerlessness. The ultimate danger of the Vampire archetype is the takeover: you become victim to a state of possession and lose your selfhood. Then, in many ways, you yourself incarnate the dysfunctional, invasive behavior and the emptiness of the Vampire.

The Vampire Transmuted

The Vampire, when Transmuted, reveals the other side of being wounded: the healing. Where the poison is kept, so too the medicine is present. The Transmuted Vampire possesses life-enhancing abilities. The generative power of the Vampire Transmuted offers the way of restoration and everlasting vitality.

The Savior/Rescuer: Martyr (Compulsivity, Pathological Provider)

Through human history, the Savior/Rescuer is that archetypal entity who rescues people from harm or saves them from something threatening. However, when you identify with the shadowed embodiment of the Savior/Rescuer, you feel the never-ending obligation to rescue people from difficult and dangerous situations. Your duty is to rescue, defend, and protect. When offered in appropriate doses, these actions are of course suitable and helpful. However, when the shadow forces take over, these actions become compulsive, and the overwhelming nature of this identity robs you of your autonomy. You are forever in the service of others. To be constantly in the role of Savior/Rescuer leads to frustration and overwhelm. Taking the world's pain upon your shoulders is a burden that costs you your self-worth. When doing good deeds goes into shadow, this Soul Companion undermines your personhood.

The Savior/Rescuer Transmuted

When Transmuted, the Savior/Rescuer figure brings the qualities of attunement and compassion. This Soul Companion knows empathy and what it means to befriend others. In the inner realms and in the everyday world, having empathy and compassion to cultivate relationships with those you meet along the way is life changing. To connect with a community of inner figures, as you experienced in your Dig, is primary. The Savior/Rescuer figure when Transmuted opens possibilities for meaningful companionship and love.

In the Company of Soul Companions

The presence of Soul Companions—Supportive and Shadow—opens access to the mysteries of the worlds behind the world. They announce themselves to you with a multitude of unknown challenges and possibilities. These figures come with both emotional pathos and innate gifts. They influence emotions, actions, and sensations in the inner sphere and the world above. As you develop the capacity, the curiosity, and the willingness to receive them, you will find the special abilities they offer to be life changing and affirming. Supportive Soul Companions offer a balm for your wounds, affirmation of your talents, and capacities to manifest your most deeply held wishes. Once befriended and Illuminated, they offer the radiance and healing energy needed to discover the potential particular to you. Shadow Soul Companions make a claim on your body and mind through distress, despair, anguish, and physical afflictions of all sorts. But when confronted and then Transmuted, they ask you to understand them.

Before turning to the next chapter, take the time to assemble your Soul Companions. You now have the tools you need to gather the persons, animals, and places that will support, protect, and guide you. Through the processes of Illumination and Transmutation, you have your allies for your deeper journey. Now that you have gathered your Soul Companions, you are ready to explore the Imagination Matrix.

Chapter 4

The Four Quadrants of the Imagination Matrix

Just below the reaches of your conscious mind, beyond the personal and collective human experience, is the Imagination Matrix. The Imagination Matrix itself is composed of the Four Quadrants: Earth, Mind, Machine, and Universe. Each quadrant has a pulse, a human quality. Each is a field of energy and experience. When these fields are working in alignment, they enhance your abilities for healing, innovation, and connection.

As your Curious Mind opens, you perceive the metapatterns in continuous motion sparking through time and space. In the beginning, you experience these creative energies moving in circular motion, generating and regenerating the human spirit. This circle of creation is familiar because it is part of your biological patterning. Your life, from beginning to end, forms a complete circle. The cycle of birth, life, death, transit, and rebirth is in the natural world around us as well.

That circular life force is an energy that propels us forward. We innately understand its creative power. We use circles for many purposes. The practice of sitting together in a talking circle or in ritual is used in settings ranging from therapeutic treatment to reconciliation, from prayer to sacred ceremony. People come together in a circle to support one another's healing and well-being. Much like an ouroboros, which is commonly depicted as a serpent or sometimes a dragon swallowing its own tail, the circle has generative powers that are universal. Historically, the ouroboros comes from Gnostic and alchemical symbology, expressing the unity of all things, material and spiritual, "which never disappear but perpetually change form in an eternal cycle of destruction and re-creation."[1]

As you move along the circle, you discover different expressions of your creativity. *The origination* is the first hint of something new, the spark. *The articulation* is the further reflection of the seed idea. *The manifestation* is making the discovery real. *Communication*, the final expression, is sharing the new innovation with the world. A Course in Miracles states: "The circle of creation has no end. Its starting and its ending are the same. But in itself, it holds the universe of all creation, without beginning and without an end."[2]

The second expression of creative energies moving through the Imagination Matrix is that of a spiral. As your Curious Mind is set in motion, your perspective shifts. The circle begins to expand outward into a spiral, as each rotation expresses a new articulation of a deeper creative imagination. This hidden energetic thread sourcing innovation and imagination operates through multiple dimensions.

In the natural world, the patterns of spirals are ever present. In modern cultures, perhaps most familiar are the spirals identified in the DNA double helix. You also recognize spiral designs in some plants and fruits, like sunflowers, pineapples, and pine cones. Or in various living creatures, like mollusk shells or the nautilus shells of sea creatures. All display a center point with a series of circular shapes revolving around it in a circular pattern. From draining water to whirlpools, from hurricanes to galaxies, spiral formations evolve. When the center turns faster than the periphery, waves within these phenomena get spun around into spirals.[3] Charlotte Sleigh, who explores the imagery of spirals and scientific innovation in visualizing new discoveries, described, "DNA is everywhere. Twisting and snaking across screens, newspaper articles, and advertisements, the double helix of DNA is an icon of our age."[4] Vibrant, alive, the movement and procreative flow of the spiral design heighten your awareness in your journeying through the realms of deep imagination.

The Imagination Matrix exists across multiple dimensions and across interactive and interconnected experiences in continuous motion. As you continue to explore the shapes, rhythms, and dimensions of imagination, you can build on what you notice in circles and spirals and extend across time and space. The concept is fundamental to both Indigenous teachings and contemporary applications of quantum physics. Dynamic circles, spirals, and cycles are the interrelated patterning of the Imagination Matrix.

Karl Pribram's holonomic brain theory (quantum holography), for example, provides evidence on how much of the mind's processing is done in "wholes,"[5] referring to the brain processing information throughout its entirety. Echoing Pribram's work, theoretical physicist David Bohm asserted that mind and matter emerge from a unified field, the "implicate order."[6] The implicate order is that which underpins all things.

The implicate order became a primary concept for me when I was conducting field research for my dissertation on dreamwork. Dream figures roam in the interconnected quantum fields of the implicate order. Bringing your awareness to this domain of consciousness, your imagination sparks. I discovered that dream images contain aspects of both mind and matter, existing in an interrelated field. This unified field of dreaming includes person, culture, world, and cosmos.[7]

Exploring the Four Quadrants

Each of the Four Quadrants informs the others with its innate knowing, and each offers you sparks of awareness that contribute to manifesting your life purpose.

Quadrant 1: Earth

Earth/Regeneration: Fertile Soil/Generativity, Rhizomic Networks/ Deep Ecology, Incarnate/Embodied, Cycle of Life/Spiral, Body/Soma, Wounding/Healing, Grounding/Belonging

Element: Earth

Earth, the first quadrant, opens you to exploration of Earth's living systems. The Earth Quadrant awakens you to nature's imagination. When you witness a caterpillar becoming a butterfly or the winter receding into spring, you experience the mystery and wonder of the life cycle. You become attuned to an animated world, to the rhythms of nature's genius playing through your life. Attention here opens your natural mind and your instinctual body, your animal body. Feeling connected in the extended family of creatures and places, you find a sympathetic attitude of engagement, becoming one of the many in the dance of life.

You experience your physical and emotional roots extending into the ground beneath. Grounding down connects you to the interrelated fields of Earth's ecosystems, Earth's body. Body to body, you open ever more fully into your experience of Gaia. Just as the interrelated root systems in a grove of redwood trees allow one tree to extend nutrients and protection to another, you experience the interdependent fields of connection existing below the surface of individual human capacity. You become part of what has become known as *the rhizomatic dimension of consciousness.*

 Working with Quadrant 1: Earth

Purpose: To tap the natural resources of Earth consciousness before engaging in the agenda of a meeting, in the dialogue of a relationship, or in any activity of consequence.

Accessing Earth awareness opens your instinctual intelligence. The animal powers of your bodily sensations heighten. Your keen sense of body wisdom expands. The abilities to discern and intuit amplify.

Process: Allow your body to be supported from the bottom up. Breathe. Imagine you are drawing the nutrients of the Earth into your entire body, like a tree does with its roots. Place two fingers on your wrist or over your heart and feel your pulse. Pause. Take the time to align with the regenerative energies moving through your body. Unplug from your devices, let go, and breathe. Notice how nature's rhythms course through you as you replace the programming of the machines with the pulse of the natural world. Both are important, of course; yet here, now, experience the instinctual capacities of your human body and harmonize with the living systems of a wider ecology.

Go on a walkabout outside, either in your backyard, city streets, or in a natural landscape. Reorient your relationship to your pace. Perhaps wander aimlessly instead of with intent. Follow Curiosity. Notice what in the landscape captivates your interest—the song of a bird, a branch moving in the wind, a flower, a butterfly—and follow where it leads. Stop here. Notice. Take another moment: write, draw, or listen to what is presenting itself to you. In addition, allow the particularity of color, shape, texture, and movement to be revealed.

Let the poetics of the scene unfold. With permission, you might bring some of what you witnessed back with you to your homeplace—colorful flowers or leaves, interesting rocks, shells, et cetera. This praxis will sustain your connection with the life force moving through Earth and through you. Take a moment to express your gratitude to the generative source from which you and all of life have originated.

As you continue your engagement with the Earth Quadrant, you can further apply the self-healing properties of Earth's regenerative nature to the physical or emotional challenges of your personal circumstances. Identify a particular issue that is causing you agitation. Give it a name and write it down on a piece of paper or an object. Next, place the paper or object among the items that you gathered in your walkabout through the natural landscape. Take a few steps back and notice how the painful experience that you have necessarily been so identified with now is part of a larger ecology. See the particularity of your personal challenge in a wider context. Breathe more deeply into the places opening in your body. Experience in your body the healing powers of Earth's (nature's) body.

Quadrant 2: Mind

Mind/Imaginal Consciousness: Mind/Soul, Depth Psychology/Soul's Realization, Mythological Motifs/Mythic Imagination, Archetypal Figures/Soul Companions, Mental Intention/Positive Expectation, Complexes/Habituated Patterns, Transformation/Individuation

Element: Air

The Mind Quadrant consists of the many dominions of the psyche. Embedded in this quadrant are the many selves within and without you. Multidimensional by nature, the pluralistic mind opens imagination beyond the monovision of the singular viewpoint. Many characters come into visibility, just as they do in a fairy tale, story, or myth. In these living images, you encounter that which exists behind your moods, symptoms, aspirations. The ideas, inhabitants, landscapes, and soul companions have a life of their own and, in turn, affect you in tangible ways. Psyche becomes a primary ground from which behavior is shaped. Story becomes the medium of exchange, and curiosity sparks continuing engagement. Throughout human experience, this quadrant has been foundational to intuition, insight, warning, and guidance.

 Working with Quadrant 2: Mind

Purpose: To engage your authentic soul's voice when it is needed or when you feel disconnected.

Your connection to the soul comes forward in the mind's eye through living embodied images. Bring awareness to your dreams, fantasies, behaviors, moods, and afflictions. You are not just an observer. Your physical body and emotional life are always expressing the soul's desire to be realized.

Process: Working with the Mind Quadrant requires mastering the skills of image-based practices. Start by identifying an image from a dream or a waking fantasy that has recently occurred to you. Close your eyes. Breathe. Allow the image to take shape in your consciousness. Next, make a sketch of the figure. The doodle need not be overly sophisticated and is not meant to be put on display. By giving form to the image, you are placing it outside of you. It then becomes possible to establish an ongoing relationship with it. Your work now is to befriend the image, the Imaginal figure or landscape. Take the time to notice the particularity of the image. What distinguishes it from other, similar figures? Are they recurrent figures for you? These are your Soul Companions.

What feeling, emotion, sensation, or desire does this image evoke in you? Write your thoughts down, then begin a dialogue with the image. In turn, let the image respond to you through its voice, on its behalf, in its own autonomy. Repeat the dialogue between you and the image several times. Write down what you hear. Sketch or paint what you see, either a depiction of the figure or the places it takes you. Build or sculpt in clay the figure or a setting it introduces you to. As you engage in dialogue, listen to the voice originating in the figure itself before responding, and notice what begins to open in you.

This is now a conversation of a different order: a dialogue of the imagining mind. During the process, bring awareness to how you are responding to your Soul Companions. Remember to breathe. Let your mind's eye expand with each breath. Something new is emerging; an expanded Imaginal consciousness is evolving. Continue in this process for some time. How is this state of being different from your habituated ways of engaging in interpersonal and intrapersonal interactions?

In addition to your ability to think more clearly, your ability to discern what is needed becomes heightened during the exercise and after. You feel a stronger connection to your authentic self and your calling. You can keep the manic buzz of modern life at the appropriate distance, and you can embrace your creative life.

Quadrant 3: Machine

Machine/Cocreation: Human/Tech Evolution, Virtual/Augmented Realities, Mechanical/Transformation, Functional/Operational, Emergence/Complexity, Chi/Energy

Element: Fire

Do machines imagine? No, they cannot. But *your* dreams and imagination enable new technologies to realize the incarnation of the never-before possible. From intricately designed surgical equipment to manufactured instruments for rocket engines, machines enhance creativity and extend capacities. Virtual and augmented realities complemented by artificial intelligence (AI) can operate as a means of extending your sensate and intellectual capabilities.

Machines, especially adaptations of virtual, augmented, and mixed reality, can facilitate creative expression. This cocreative relationship offers the promise of extending curiosity and innovation beyond personal limitations to enhance the human collective. Of course, too much reliance on machines or excessive screen time dims the Curious Mind. Rather than fearing the takeover by the machine, it is important to remember that new technologies need your imagination to sustain their development.

 Working with Quadrant 3: Machine

Purpose: To access your Curious Mind when you feel like the world is becoming too robotic, mechanized, or algorithmically driven.

New technologies enhance attunement with your Curious Mind when used in complementary, not oppositional, ways. The emergence of augmented realities brings the possibility of using technology as a tool—not a substitute—for increased presence in relationships.

Process: Take a break from your device. Before you log back on to it, slow down and open your Curious Mind. Notice what is sparking inside of you. Now open your device. What captivates your attention? Follow the thread spontaneously, without feeling the need to make a contact, buy something, or respond in any way. Sustain your presence and fascination. You are now opening to a different quality of engagement with the networks of cybertechnologies. Take the time to allow what is coming forward to deepen the actuality of your embodied experience. Design one action that you can take on behalf of this new cocreative awareness.

Practice this exercise a few times. Make a log of these activities.

The concept of fasting from devices is already taking hold organically as educational, institutional, and home environments grapple with creating generative participation with new technology. Many school districts are giving students days off from using their devices. No-cell-phone zones are being created in schools to lessen the constant social media overload.

In Silicon Valley, executives of tech firms are hiring "nature walkers" to accompany employees on excursions into natural places like the mountains, beaches, and parks. No devices allowed. They are also suggesting employees go for digital detox retreats.[8] This is viewed as a reboot.

Quadrant 4: Universe

Universe/Numinous Perception: Transcendent Experience/Cosmic Awareness, Quantum Energy/Potency, Wonder/Mystery, Intuition/Illumination, Knowledge/Connection, Belief/Destiny

Element: Spirit

The Fourth Quadrant, Universe, opens your perception into the numinous. The numinous experience lives behind and beyond your curiosity. It refers to your quality of presence and your fascination with the hints of nonegoic powers existing in the cosmos. Your numinous experiences have a quasi-mystical nature: they link you to that spark of mystery at the center of creation.

Wisdom teachers and Indigenous healers have been in touch with the numinous since the beginning. Their knowledge reveals the intimate connection between us and the transcendent fields of the wider cosmos. Whether you discover this connection in the configurations of the stars, in the hexagrams of the I Ching, by throwing the bones, or through using any one of countless other mediums, in this quadrant the call of the future becomes revealed in the numinous hints originating in the Imagination Matrix. As you become increasingly aware of these numinous hints, patterns emerge. The wider harmonic fields of these patterns tell of your calling and offer a glimpse of your becoming, your destiny.

As you continue your exploration and Shift Contexts, you, too, open access to the numinous. As you have experienced when moving from the rational mind to the Curious Mind, here, too, the worldview changes—nothing less than a change in cosmology. You become aware of the soul spark embedded in the creatures, landscapes, and things with which you interact. You find yourself placed right in the wonder of a universal dance.

Working with Quadrant 4: Universe

Purpose: To access the depth and breadth of the universal pulse underpinning all being when you need to infuse life with purpose, spiritual balance, or a sense of the numinous.

Process: Begin with Shifting Context. This can be as functional as changing your routine from working inside the home to finding an office place outside the house. Or you might take spacious time to listen to the sounds of nature, feel the wind on your skin, or notice the glow of a sunrise or sunset. If you have the opportunity, gaze at the stars in their nightly movements. In these experiences, you are gaining a sense of the shift from solar to lunar consciousness.

Another path to the numinous might be to experience a simple object through a different mode of perception—the process of seeing the universe in a grain of sand. For example, take time each day for several days in a row to let a very small object, like a leaf, pine cone, or stone, captivate your curiosity. Take fifteen minutes each day to bring your acute perception to the object. Notice the intricacies, the textures, the internal coherence of what you are perceiving. Allow the universe, the macro, to reveal itself in the micro.

As you engage in these warm-up experiences, take note of what opens inside of you. How does your breathing change, what is it like to slow down, what shifts of consciousness occur as you take in a bigger picture? From here, make a list. Identify what interests, desires, tasks create inspiration. Write them down or make a sketch that represents each. While doing so, notice which intimations, hints, begin to Illuminate. The excitement, even passion, that gets stimulated offers reliable feedback as to your authentic desires and the unique path that is yours to walk.

The Confluence

In the Imagination Matrix, the elements of the Four Quadrants are always in motion. I call these points of connection the *Confluence*: the ever-generating birthplace of the new possible. The energetic threads of Earth, Mind, Machine, and Universe fuse at multiple points of Confluence. Each Confluence provides the energy that births inspiration and engenders innovation.

The qualities derived from the elements of the Four Quadrants make up your *Imaginal Intelligence*, which ignites your creative potential. But how do you tap into it and use its power? In the next chapter, you will learn how to use the limitless resources in the Imagination Matrix to up your Imaginal IQ.

Chapter 5

Imaginal Intelligence

Over the years, I have found that when people open their Curious Mind and connect to the Four Quadrants of the Imagination Matrix, their Imaginal Intelligence increases. There are many kinds of intelligence—intellectual, emotional, and physiological, to name but a few. Imaginal Intelligence is the capacity to utilize the insights from the multiplicity of forces that inform all things seen and unseen. These supercharged sparks are generated by the many interconnected points of the Imagination Matrix. Like the genetic messages located in your biological DNA, you are encoded with an Imaginal Intelligence. Looking at the night sky, you are reminded that there is always a bigger picture, a macro system forever moving, of which you are a particular part. This Imaginal Intelligence is alive in each of us. We experience the expanded imagination as a kind of inheritance.

Imaginal Intelligence is embedded in our genetic dispositions from birth. We witness its awakening when we see a one-year-old instinctively seeking a smile, then responding with a gesture or sound. A child's ability to engage imagination via multiple modes increases exponentially from there. At one and a half, vocabulary begins to increase tenfold; by two we can glimpse pattern formation and conceptual perception. Next come abilities to extrapolate, to play interpersonally, even to manipulate an iPhone! By age four, the capacity to play beginners' board games opens. The innate talent to make up or listen to stories of imagination is in full swing.

Early childhood is the homeplace for Imaginal Intelligence. It is where you first engage in Imaginal Play. However, as traditional education progresses through the elementary school years, children become more and more disconnected from the natural mind. In the standard curriculum, cultivating Imaginal Intelligence is replaced by methodologies of teaching to the test.

Reconnecting with Your Imaginal Intelligence

How can you reconnect to and enhance Imaginal Intelligence to meet the personal and collective challenges/opportunities of our times? You must first access your body's instinctual knowledge and somatic wisdom for self-healing. There is a reciprocal relationship between Imaginal Intelligence and body wisdom. Shifting Context between the micro and the macro, as you have done in your Dig experiences between the worldview and the cosmic view, opens your reception. As your awareness of your somatic experience grows, your Imaginal Intelligence enlivens. As your body relaxes and your life force flows, your breath deepens and your heart warms. Getting a larger perspective sparks creativity. Space is opened for the unexpected, for intuition, and for abstraction.

For example, when Craig enrolled in an artist workshop for beginners, he noticed something unexpected. Equipped with paints, brushes, and an easel, he began to paint spontaneously to the mood of the music that the instructor was playing. He allowed himself to just be present in the experience, as he had when he was a young boy. He let his hands and the brushes, even the paints themselves, give expression to the music moving through his body. He noticed his breath deepening and, soon, his curiosity awakening. He felt his imagination coming to life, as if he were moving from a world of black and white to one of glorious high-definition color. As the images came to him, his Imaginal Intelligence expanded. He was able to see things he had never seen before—designs, patterns, and even objects. He left the workshop different from when he had entered: more open, more attuned to the people and things around him.

Beth also experienced something unexpected when she opened herself up to her Imaginal Intelligence. She and her partner had just purchased their first home. The home had a small, unkempt backyard. Beth felt called to bring life and vitality to this neglected space. Though she had never planted a garden before, she decided to give it a go. She first went online to gather information and then went to the nursery to obtain plants, tools, and the nutrients that she would need to get started. The nursery, filled with the fragrances and colors of an abundance of plants, was a revelatory experience. She was filled with curiosity, some intimidation, and wonder, too. The combination of earth, planting instructions, gardening tools, and faith in the generative life cycle of nature captured Beth's creative interest. As the days went forward, Beth experienced something more. She was part of the vast and interconnected world around her. This sparked an elevated sense of purpose and understanding. Her imagination enlivened, and her Imaginal Intelligence increased.

Neuroplasticity and Imaginal Intelligence

Science is discovering that the brain continues to grow and change throughout your life span. Neuroplasticity can change the brain's design—how it responds to experience—by reorganizing connections via so-called wiring and rewiring. This ability can be channeled in ways that are positive or detrimental.[1]

And, too, there are particularized ways of measuring each of these aptitudes: IQ tests, emotional intelligence inventories, and various instruments to assess physiological responses, all designed to calculate and then quantify your abilities in a given area. These scores measure your standing in comparison to others, provide criteria upon which to set goals, and signal deficiencies when scores drop. Universities and other institutions gather intellectual intelligence (IQ) data for purposes of admissions and/or placement. Therapists use emotional intelligence (EI) scores to develop enhancement and treatment strategies. Physicians use data from physiological testing to provide you with a comprehensive health evaluation (diagnosis and treatment protocols). Overall, mental, emotional, and physical aptitude measurements play an important role. The outcomes of these systems of measurement are meant to provide guidance for conducting your life.

Research on neuroplasticity in the child's brain reveals that as you become more technologically dependent, the capacity to imagine spatially gets reduced.[2] In other words, we imagine less, think more, and become better adapted to follow the programmer's code. The innate wiring of your natural mind, the place of curiosity and imagination, yields to a more robotic, scientific mind, providing the means to process bits of information at an accelerated pace. The neural networks of the brain change size and shape to accommodate. As you get caught up in the fast-paced whirl of ceaseless tasks and endless screen time, our capacity to slow down and engage Imaginal Intelligence becomes limited or extinguished altogether. Imaginal Intelligence is replaced by artificial intelligence. Stagnation replaces plasticity. But new findings in neurophysiology demonstrate that increased theta networks in the brain counter this trend with measurable increases in the capacities for creativity, innovation, and imagination.[3] How do you cultivate, not lose, the capabilities of your Imaginal Intelligence?

The Imagination Matrix holds the key. The Four Quadrants, in Confluence, work together to enhance your capacities. The Four Quadrants plus Imaginal Intelligence make up the system I call *IQ4*.

 Receiving Insights from the Quadrants: IQ4

Earth. Opening to ecological awareness has a direct and foundational impact on increasing your Imaginal IQ. Being in wonder about nature opens your capacity for curiosity and awe. Each of us has coded in our DNA a bit of nature's genius. Witnessing the ingenuity of nature's creations amplifies your own creative instinct.

Mind. Engaging and evolving your relationships with the Soul Companions will also have a tremendous impact on your Imaginal IQ. Read through your notes from your journeys in your Dig and notice what images and stories once again captivate your curiosity. Create time for your own figures of imagination to emerge and spontaneously tell their stories. You can do the same with images from a nighttime dream or a daytime dreamlike experience. As their intelligence opens and is heard, your Imaginal aptitude becomes stronger.

Machine. Moving toward, not away from, new technologies—particularly in augmented, mixed, and mirrored realities—can also expand your Imaginal IQ. Meeting cyberreality with a Curious Mind, not only operational expertise, can open access to valuable tools for navigating imagination. Something different occurs. You experience the Imaginal Intelligence that originated the programming.

Universe. Changing your perspectives by Shifting Context, you experience what Illuminates in and on the landscape. Perceiving your life and those around you through the lens of the cosmos reminds you that you are one part of a beautiful, perpetually moving universe. This act of Imaginal Intelligence boosts your abilities to think and dream in innovative and unexpected ways.

Cultivating Imaginal Intelligence

Mindful meditation has become well-known over the past few decades in the West. From yoga studios to meditation centers, from in-home practices to large group experiences, many people have explored meditation in multiple ways.[4] Whatever the particular form, the time set aside to separate from the business and other demands of modern life has become integral to self-care. Study after study has demonstrated that when in a meditative state, the body relaxes, and the mind calms.[5] Brainwave activity begins to shift from an internalized mind's wandering and distracted alpha state to a more creative and reflective theta rhythm. The ego-driven mind slows down. Space opens for a restorative quality of present-centeredness.

Mindful meditation uses time-honored techniques to quiet the busy mind. In contrast, journeying in the deep imagination opens the Curious Mind. Numinous imagery comes forward. As this experience unfolds, brain wave activity shifts from the alpha state to the theta state. Research demonstrates that theta brain wave activity increases as your journey through deep imagination continues, and so does your Imaginal Intelligence.

Increasing Theta Waves

When you journey in deep imagination, the brain doesn't care if the images that come forward are real or not. Whether you see a physical tree in your yard or an Imaginal tree in your mind, the brain behaves in similar ways. The key is to look at both with a Curious Mind. When you pay attention to visual information in the environment, the alpha activity in the back of the head naturally decreases. The same effect happens when you let yourself "see" something in deep imagination—a person, animal, landscape, Soul Companion—as if it were real and right in front of you.

What this does in your brain is to drop alpha waves (thinking, ego) and raise theta waves (universal awareness). This is the crossover point where theta becomes higher than alpha. And this is the state in which you access the deep imagination and your Imaginal Intelligence.

This state can feel like the twilight state just before sleep. The trick is not to fall asleep, but to stay in this sweet spot, where you gain access to your Imaginal Intelligence, for as long as you can. Sustaining this state of consciousness can be encouraged and explored by rewarding theta activity (4–8 Hz) in the back of the head while decreasing alpha (8–12 Hz) activity in the same location. There have been several research studies of alpha-theta training with creatives in different fields of the arts. Getting to the theta state seems to enhance people's artistic expression and innovation.[6]

Shifting to Theta

You may need to repeat this next exercise several times to properly shift out of alpha and hold the state of theta. If your mind moves into some form of analysis, you've slipped out of the theta state of consciousness, and alpha has taken over. Interestingly, the same praxis I describe here has been used in numerous research studies to help individuals suffering from PTSD.[7] In essence, being in theta teaches people to transfer attention outside of themselves, disrupting many of the ruminative processes that frequently occur with a variety of mental health issues.

Journeying in the Imagination Matrix by increasing theta brain activity can be accomplished in two ways: with eyes open and with eyes closed. Each offers a method for you to sustain theta.

Increasing Theta: Eyes Open/Attention Outward

Create space. Find a thirty-minute block of time when you can be without external demands or distractions. Separate from screens of any kind and from agendas of daily tasks.

Perceive. Locate yourself in nature or look through a window where you can perceive such a place.

Find your center. Take five minutes to breathe and center yourself in a way that works for you. Experience a flow with increased presence.

Witness. In this state of heightened mindfulness, bring a witnessing presence to the natural place you are in or are perceiving through the window.

Follow Curiosity. Let your Curious Mind, not your rational mind, be your guide. Experience being inside your surroundings, not separate from them. When thoughts come into your mind, let them pass like clouds in the sky. Feel the rhythm of the landscape.

Immerse. Continue your experience here for as long as feels right to you, inviting in this quality of new consciousness.

Return. Take time to stretch and allow yourself slowly and peacefully to come back into your body and your everyday world.

The second two words approach to increase theta brain wave activity through accessing the Imagination Matrix uses sound to guide your mind inward, allowing your subconscious to be disinhibited, open, and spacious. To do this praxis with eyes closed, you wear headphones for audio feedback. The exercise often requires thirty to forty minutes, during which you become very relaxed. You simply allow the feedback to guide the mind into the realms of deep imagination.

Increasing Theta: Eyes Closed/Attention Inward

Begin. Choose a piece of music you find calming. It is best for this exercise if there are no lyrics, which can be distracting. Turn the music on and close your eyes. Start the practice by slowing down and becoming aware of your breathing.

Breathe. As you have practiced before, send your breath down through your chest into your stomach. Imagine that your feet have roots at the bottom that reach down through the floor, then into the earth, even if you are on a second story or higher. Breathe. Allow the music to flow through you.

Go into your Dig. Find your portal and journey through the realms of deep imagination. Invite your Soul Companions to come forward. Let go. Become part of this Imaginal ecology of places and figures.

Follow Curiosity. Continue your experience in this new consciousness for as long as possible.

Return. Use your Dig process to return safely to the everyday world.

Researching Imaginal Intelligence

Is there a way in which we can further measure that the praxis of journeying in the Imagination Matrix increases theta waves and raises Imaginal Intelligence? To find out, I reached out to Divergence Neuro Technology Inc., a neurotech company based in Toronto. Their mission is to develop applications for enriching mental health and cognitive performance. They have designed a new feedback technology to enhance self-awareness and brain health. As their founder, Alex Ni, describes, "We are deeply grounded in the belief that applied neuroscience, when combined with cloud, AI, and mobility, will bring positive and meaningful advances for mental health care."[8] Divergence Neuro Technology equips therapists with a remote, cloud-based neurofeedback platform so they can improve patient outcomes. The platform helps clients increase their mental health by making at-home neurofeedback practice accessible. When the company offered to let me try it out, I welcomed the opportunity. I worked with an esteemed and experienced practitioner, Dr. Jeff Tarrant, a licensed psychologist, board certified in neurofeedback, who is the director of the NeuroMeditation Institute.

The Crown

At first, I was put off by the idea of wearing yet another machine designed to monitor my body and spew more digital data for feedback. Seriously, when they offered me the "crown," as the headset was named, I almost turned and walked away. However, the promise that I could test my hypothesis that Imaginal Intelligence could be measured was too great to resist. Would this simple, elegant device be the means to do this?

For well over forty years, I have experienced the healing powers of the deep imagination. It is my life's work. But never before has this type of journeying been measured or used to increase theta. This would be a first. So the game was on. I would test the machine. I followed the prescribed protocol, which has had success with using music to help foster a meditative state. All the transmitters sent information about my brain's activity back to a screen for me to see. After the first ten minutes of wearing the crown, I felt a subtle change. Now, I wanted to test my hypothesis. Would the same protocol and adding the Dig to open deep imagination spike my theta state as well? In this way, we would be able to measure the Imagining mind.

I closed my eyes and entered the Dig. I journeyed where the Soul Companions make their travels and into the realms of deep imagination as I know them. The results were immediate. When I opened my eyes and glanced at the screen, my theta state had increased a full 88 percent. The device had previously measured increased meditative states, but never had it measured the imagining mind—until now. Here was the first empirical proof.

Measuring the Imagining Mind

The empirical proof that the crown provided was a breakthrough in showing the power of the imagining mind. We now are on the cutting edges of technologies that can help us measure our Imaginal IQ and the techniques to boost it. I believe developing a measurement tool and providing outcome information regarding aptitude in Imaginal Intelligence can be as useful as, if not more than, other diagnostic systems. I have witnessed this correspondence time and again in thousands of people with whom I have worked worldwide.

As you have read, I have designated Imaginal Intelligence as IQ4, bringing emphasis to an Imaginal Intelligence that evolves from the Four Quadrants. Now, working with a team of research experts from the fields of neurophysiology, psychology, phenomenology, and ecology, we have developed both qualitative (subjective) and quantitative (empirical) research protocols that measure Imaginal Intelligence. These pioneering research tools make assessments and provide outcome information. Measuring Imaginal Intelligence and gathering reliable post-evaluation data provide the information needed to develop particularized programs and processes to increase IQ4. I have commissioned a groundbreaking two-pronged neuroscientific study with the Academy of Imagination, an innovation center and think tank I founded in Santa Barbara, California, in 2019. The intent is to bring this work, underpinned by academic discipline, into further public and private use. We have some exciting preliminary findings.

The Quantitative Study

Early indications of the quantitative study affirm that engagement in deep imagination creates a measurable shift in our state of consciousness. As IQ4 grows, neuroplasticity increases and new brain networks develop. In other words, a new consciousness evolves. Trials working with the crown headset have repeatedly demonstrated that after a brief period of centering and once the mind is inside the experience of the Dig, theta brain activity increases. Time spent in the experience of journeying through deep imagination was accompanied by increased theta activity (4–8 Hz) in the back of the head. During this period, alpha activity (8–12 Hz) decreased in the same location. When the theta patterns become stronger than the alpha patterns— the crossover point—Imaginal consciousness is engaged. For those unfamiliar with this state, it can take multiple sessions to achieve this quality of consciousness and maintain it for longer than a few minutes. For people who have become familiar with the practice of the Dig or its equivalent, achieving and maintaining theta consciousness happens more spontaneously.

The Qualitative Study

The qualitative research was conducted by highly regarded academic research scholars with subjects who had been practicing deepening their experience with dreams and imagination for over three years in my certificate training programs. Students of deep imagination from three different levels of yearlong training participated in the study. Each responded to 193 multiple-choice rankings and ten open narrative questions. Initial research findings clustered in three themes: accessibility, creativity, and transformation. We gathered rich descriptions of the experiences and transformative potential of tending imagination. This qualitative research measured increases and key takeaways of Imaginal Intelligence.

With this study in hand, it is possible to further substantiate that Imaginal Intelligence can be both amplified and applied in concrete ways. By journeying in the realms of deep imagination, subjects reported that their Imaginal Intelligence increased. Imaginal Intelligence can expand many aspects of personal and professional life.

Access to Imagination Deepens

Participants reported that by journeying in the realms of deep imagination, they experienced a substantial increase in their ability to access Imaginal Intelligence. The more time spent in the Imagination Matrix, the more they were able to locate openings, or portals, to expand Imaginal insight. This boost in Imaginal Intelligence led them to experience a sense of "a generative dynamism below the surface of things."[9] Thus the research showed a correlation between journeying in the realms of deep imagination and increasing Imaginal Intelligence.

Creativity and Innovation Increases

The quantitative research validated the findings of the qualitative study: Imaginal Intelligence generates an increase in creativity, innovation, ingenuity, and out-of-the-box thinking. Participants who journeyed in the realms of deep imagination were able to innovate more effectively. As Imaginal Intelligence increased, they reported feeling a greater sense of wonder, which opened them to enhanced curiosity and awe. Many of the highest findings related to confirming the growth of creativity. Creative thinking and creative cognition improved. The drive for exploration and new knowledge was boosted. Participants reported that their awakened Imaginal Intelligence led to new bursts of innovation in their daily lives and work.

Theta Networks Build

Many participants commented on how engaged imagination kick-started a meaningful transformative process for them. In this context, those in the study reported a connection to nature's flow and enhanced transformative consciousness. Participants felt "more attuned to the rhythms of nature" because of the work. A bodily experience of Illuminated Consciousness was one of the most significant increases reported across the three years of training: as Imaginal Intelligence increased, so too did access to the body's wisdom. Across all years of training, emotional resilience and relational connection, as well as health and healing benefits, emerged in the research. The study also found a strong correlation between upticks in Imaginal Intelligence and greater feelings of well-being.

The ability to measure deep imagination and its relationship to Imaginal Intelligence is an exciting breakthrough. Imaginal Intelligence is a very important addition to other understandings of intelligence. The work of imagination and dreaming, with its qualities of deepening and slowing time, builds theta networks in the brain. Mixed-methods research with both quantitative and qualitative approaches demonstrated that the praxis of the Dig and journeying in deep imagination enhances theta, the state of Imaginal Intelligence.

The Promise

Based on the results from these quantitative and qualitative studies, we have deepened our research. Our findings have been consistent. Increasing Imaginal Intelligence does interface with other aptitudes: creativity is enhanced, and intellectual acuity is positively impacted. When your Imaginal Intelligence increases, your curiosity opens, your worldview widens, your ability to innovate amplifies, and your overall quality of life improves.

I believe that Imaginal Intelligence, IQ4, can take a central position in curriculum planning, business practices, and personal development programs in the future. We are at the beginning of understanding how to measure, evaluate, and create new programs informed by reliable findings. From these early studies, four qualitative dimensions of Imaginal Intelligence present themselves for future research: *how Imaginal Intelligence enhances well-being, deepens creativity, increases innovation, and awakens transformation.* It is my conviction that Imaginal Intelligence must take its place in the pantheon of intelligences, including emotional intelligence and more. As is verified by this research, we are now able to reinforce and increase Imaginal Intelligence. Doing so will impact nothing short of the next evolution of human consciousness.

As your Imaginal Intelligence grows, you can access something more. In the next chapter you will discover the gift or gifts that are uniquely yours to unwrap. Imaginal Intelligence gives birth to your Innate Genius, waiting to be known.

Chapter 6

Discovering Your Innate Genius

Each of us, all eight billion, come into the world similar in our basic structure: bones, blood, skin, organs. Yet each of us is a one-off. From the unimaginable number of possible genetic combinations, you are birthed into your physiological uniqueness. There is no one else quite the same as you. You evolve with a unique inheritance, a birthright that carries the seeds of your *Innate Genius*.

People ask me, "Can everybody be a 'genius'? Isn't this a term used for the very exceptional few?"

It is true that over the course of human history, we have called certain individuals who seem to operate at a quantum leap ahead of their time "genius." We assume that such acuity is out of reach for the rest of us. But what if that assumption is simply not the case—what if it is too limited?

I believe what sources Imaginal Intelligence is, in fact, the same as what holds your Innate Genius. This is the Imagination Matrix. As you learned in the last chapter, when the elements of the Four Quadrants intersect and come into Confluence, your Imaginal Intelligence increases. So too does your ability to discover your Innate Genius. The people whom we think of as being geniuses have found the way to activate their calling to its highest potential. You can too.

Your Innate Genius, the creative force moving within you, is yours alone to manifest. Your Innate Genius is waiting to be realized and takes on many expressions: creating a beautiful garden, preparing an exceptional meal, organizing a distinguished business, being a caring parent, helping someone become the best version of themselves. Your genius need not be something that manifests with great fanfare or has an impact on a global level. When embodying your Innate Genius, you are securely placed in your humility, not flying high in grandiosity.

Your Innate Genius asks to be expressed in tangible ways. It is not a hidden treasure, designed to be kept from view or use. Following the methods of journeying into the realms of deep imagination, you will find what you need to engage and align with your Innate Genius. The task ahead is an applied one, practical by nature. The goal is simple and achievable. The exercises that follow add to your existing repertoire of skills and bring focus to the process of accessing your Innate Genius.

But first, a word of caution. Once you start down this path, there is no turning back. Though you have had glimpses of your Innate Genius throughout your life, it is easier to push these away, numb yourself to their potency, when they are only quick peeks. However, as your Innate Genius comes more fully into view, its sheer force leaves little choice but to accept your calling. To do otherwise leads to trouble.

Much of your turmoil, which can sometimes be expressed as neurosis or worse, often comes from ignoring, separating from, or sublimating your Innate Genius. The consequences can be dire. A life divorced from its purpose, from its soul-centered destiny, can feel empty. These are the preconditions for various kinds of chemical abuse and mental/emotional disturbance. To avoid this outcome, reconnect with your courage and resolve. Begin by making a personal resolution: "At this time in my life I will summon my courage to follow my dream, my Innate Genius, and fulfill my destiny." When you are in service to your Innate Genius, the beauty of your life's purpose awakens. You experience love and a passion for your work in the world. As the poet Rumi says, "Let the beauty you love be what you do."[1]

I have found that there are three main conditions for doing this work: One, necessity. Two, courage. Three, curiosity.

Necessity often inspires change and the motivation to work through adversity. It takes *courage* to mobilize your mettle. It takes time and practice. Starting each day with your Dig, through the Imagination Matrix, activates your *courage* and once again helps you to follow your *curiosity*. You are now able to overcome fear and embrace your authentic self. I do not want to simplify this key outcome. To achieve this result in an ongoing way takes work, perseverance, and dedication.

Harvesting the Seeds of Innate Genius

The concept of Innate Genius has actually been with us through the millennia. The philosophers and poets, artists and scientists of previous generations expressed their Innate Genius in works that have come down to us through the centuries. However, our personal connection to that seed impulse has diminished in the distractions and speed of the modern age. When you pay attention, you realize that forces greater than you move through your perceptions and behavior. As Michael Meade said, "The genius inside a person wants activity. It's connected to the stars; it's connected to a spark and it wants to burn and it wants to make and it wants to create and it has gifts to give. That is the nature of inner genius."[2]

Finding your Innate Genius comes not as a sudden flash, but as a sustained awareness of the hints generated by your connection to Imaginal Intelligence. We often ignore these subtle inflections because issues of daily life, such as finishing school or finding work, become more imperative. Yet the seeds remain alive inside of you, ready to grow. These hints might surface in your dreams or at times when you feel broken down. The seeds of your Innate Genius can be found in the questions you ask yourself in despair: *Why am I here? What am I good at? Is there anything about my life that is worthwhile?* It is by allowing yourself to examine what lives underneath that you begin to recognize your Innate Genius.

This happened with Fred. Fred worked steadily in his job as a manager at a construction company. He enjoyed his crew and their projects and was proud to provide a good lifestyle for his family. However, Fred felt increasingly frustrated. The routine of his work was wearing him down. He felt stuck.

That brought Fred to one of my workshops. Since organizational skills came easily to him, he liked the assignment to identify and track the flashes of new perceptions and ideas that might come in the course of his daily activities. He began writing them down in a notebook along with design features that caught his eye each day. Fred kept this journal next to the blueprints, construction guidelines, and permit documents that were part of his daily routine. Keeping his Curious Mind open to the seeds of Innate Genius, he gradually filled the notebook.

After six months, he took a few days off to spend time reading through what he gathered, without other distractions. The bigger picture revealed itself to him. He recognized that the lure he felt about the construction business and working with his hands had begun back in middle school, in a woodshop class. In fact, he loved everything about making fine objects out of wood. This craft had always called to him, and he knew he needed to switch his focus. Within one year, fueled by the passion of his Innate Genius, Fred became a finish carpenter with a thriving business.

Beth worked as a nurse at one of the best hospitals in Arizona. She had felt called to the nursing profession. She loved her job, even when the pandemic required her to work almost around the clock. She knew that she truly helped many people. Yet Beth still felt something was missing in her life. She was not at all clear what these feelings were about. But having a stable income to support her children, she was reluctant to rock the boat.

Through participating in one of my online programs, Beth used the same process as Fred had undergone. Beginning with paying attention to the hints, the inflections of what came her way in her daytime experience and nighttime dreams, she discovered that she was really attracted to the music played to ease patients' anxiety in the hospice unit. The patients loved this, and so did Beth. She noticed that she loved singing at night to her children and when alone in the shower. Beth remembered that she had participated in high school and college choral groups. Many had noted her exceptional voice. This talent, once a part of her life, had gone by the wayside as she pursued other goals. Now Beth felt the yearning of this call, and it inspired an idea. Fueled by her two passions, singing and nursing, she found the courage to approach the hospital administration. Eighteen months later, Beth was overseeing a singing therapy program she created together with the hospital. She brought music to patients in hospice and those undergoing other forms of treatments. The beauty of the sound seemed to uplift their spirits and help in their healing process.

Foundational Template: Cultivating Innate Genius

You can cultivate the seeds of your Innate Genius by following these steps:

Begin. Go through the portal you have cultivated in your Dig to the realms of deep imagination. Notice where you find yourself. What landscape are you in? Bring awareness to what is happening in the landscape and inside in your body and emotions.

Open your Curious Mind. Slow down and move from your rational mind into your Curious Mind. Filter out extraneous thoughts and noises. Invite your wonder to come forward. Experience your empathetic heart and feel more deeply.

Imagine. Think of your Innate Genius as an entity outside of yourself, in the room along with you. What color is it? What shape does it have? Notice its activity. Follow Curiosity. What or who is present? As the image of your Innate Genius changes form and motion, sustain your curiosity.

Witness. Bring a witnessing presence to the emerging details of what has come to represent your Innate Genius. As the figure continues to evolve, your curiosity continues to increase. In this process of personifying, as the seeds of your Innate Genius continue to reveal themselves, your authentic self, too, regenerates.

Find a meaningful object. Locate an object in the world that depicts aspects of what is unfolding. Place the object someplace where you can continue your engagement with it over several days.

Draw. Give expression to your call through sketching or doodling, not writing. Bring attention to the emergent patterns.

Yield. Take all the time you need and allow the Innate Genius that is surfacing to find its expression.

Repeat. This praxis can be done over and over until the hints and inflections become clear to you.

Wonders Everywhere

It is a wondrous thing to be surprised by the unexpected. Even more extraordinary is the experience of being greeted, then mirrored from the inside out, by that unanticipated place or person. I experienced precisely this kind of turn of events when I had the opportunity to meet one of the most noted painters in China, Fanzhi Zeng. His story is one of humility. Given life circumstances and limitations, he had little choice but to follow the hints of his Innate Genius, not knowing where they would lead. Step by step, without fanfare or acclaim, Fanzhi Zeng, with the support of his loving sister, Fanhui Zeng, followed the path less traveled.[3]

While in China on a lecture tour, I received a rare invitation to view his private work. Navigating through the maze and density of city traffic, rattled by the noise and speed of modern urban Chinese life, my companions and I arrived in a suburban neighborhood. Behind arched gates was the quiet of a traditional Chinese garden, with a home near the back. Inside, occupying downstairs and most of the upstairs, was the artist's studio.

Our first steps into the studio revealed more than a place in which to paint. We walked into a living sanctuary where study, contemplation, music, and meditation opened an Imaginal space. On the walls and spread on the floors, paintings filled the rooms with their living presence, revealing both their being and their becoming. The overall ambiance of the studio was spacious, welcoming, and warm, with sofa, end tables, and dining area creating a sensation of home.

Standing in front of an unfinished painting, I felt pushed to my edges, met by a force that literally took my breath away. *What is going on?* I asked myself. It was as if I was being commanded to take heed of the claim being placed on my body and soul. I realized that this painting was not a static replication of something familiar. No, in the intricacy of the many painted layers, something more, something other was pressing through. I was in awe. I was afraid. In each brushstroke and between the lines, I saw generative impulses, hints of the possible. As the hours went by, I felt that I was no longer an observer of the painting. Rather, I was surrounded by the whole of what emerged from the canvas.

Master Fanzhi Zeng walked into the room. He saw me absorbed in his painting. He then shared with me that the process of creating a painting was that of a vision being orchestrated from the inside. The painting emerged from a deep source that seemed to have its own life.[4] It was as if not only the painting itself but also the *act* of painting were an expression of his Innate Genius. When your presence greets psyche and your actions greet image, the deeper stories manifest through you. Listening to Master Fanzhi Zeng describe his artistic process and taking spacious time to deepen my relationship with several of his paintings opened a new awareness and appreciation of the eruption occurring inside of my own life and work.

For me, as for each of you, taking journeys through the Imagination Matrix opens new modes of perception and abilities to express that which is beyond the known. Each of you, in your own way, can become a master artist—an active participant in the creation of your life.

When this happens, your vision widens, your curiosity awakens, and the powers of imagination in and around you shine brightly. You develop a more expansive way of perceiving and knowing. Think of looking up to the night sky. When it is visible, you may even be privileged to see the Milky Way, the galaxy that contains our solar system. However, this is but one galaxy among the many of a limitless universe: a vast field of stars coexisting in an intergalactic web of unfathomable proportion. When you become open in this way, you allow, at least for a time, the intelligence of the living universe to inform your Innate Genius. You are part of something bigger than what you know and deeper than what you can comprehend with narrow vision.

As I experienced Master Fanzhi Zeng's paintings in his studio that day, the seeds of my Innate Genius blossomed and came to the fore-front, opening the portal to my own artistic vision. My calling as an explorer of the Imaginal realms was affirmed. As Maya Angelou wrote, "Everything in the universe has a rhythm, everything dances."[5]

❁ Expanding Your Modes of Perception: The Quick Shift Protocol

As I learned from Fanzhi Zeng, it is important to practice changing perspective to see the unseen. One way to make this shift is to view the world as an artistic landscape. To do so, you must master the ways of shuttling between *soft eyes* and *focused eyes*.

Soft eyes. With soft eyes, you widen your gaze and at first see your surroundings as the bigger picture. Like Fanzhi Zeng, you start with a perception of the background.

Focused eyes. Next, with focused eyes, you take in the particulars. Notice in detail what is literally present and, too, what is emerging from the yet-to-be-seen broader milieu that exists behind the scenes.

Point of view. Notice that as your perspectives change, you, too, experience changes. New images come forward, the invisibles make a showing, and surprises captivate your attention. As the unexpected reveals itself, your imagination is activated. In this field of dynamic perception, the artistry of your Innate Genius becomes visible and ready to be actualized.

Commitment to Yourself: Actualizing Your Innate Genius

When you express your Innate Genius, you not only fulfill your purpose but also contribute to the well-being of others. You pay it forward, so to speak. Your curiosity elevates, and the world becomes your own artistic landscape. Actualizing your Innate Genius might take time; it is meant to be practiced again and again.

Start by setting an intention: "I will bring a Curious Mind to my reflective practice of actualizing my Innate Genius." Say this intention out loud. Then write it down and tape it to the refrigerator door or bathroom mirror. Choose a time of the day where you can be alone and quiet. Set aside paper or a journal for this purpose. Light a candle or sit in nature.

Notice. Now, in your mind's eye, put on a new pair of Imaginal glasses with lenses able to see into the many worlds behind the visible world. Allow yourself to experience a particular time and place where you journeyed in the realms of deep imagination, an experience where the spaciousness and intrigue of Imaginal play held you in its fascination.

Be present. Take the time to hear the sounds of the Imaginal field that resonate with each breath. You are no longer the determiner but the receiver, yielding to another source of intelligence that exists around you and in you. Listen to what the world's soul is calling forth from you. What is being asked of your Innate Genius now?

Feel. Allow yourself to feel throughout your body what has viscerally come through to you. Place your hands wherever sensations manifest for you: heart, belly, legs. This is your touchstone, the embodied location of your Innate Genius. I have found that this praxis yields remarkable results in clarifying what the world calls us to do and be at this time.

Act. Repeat this praxis as much as needed as part of your commitment to expressing your Innate Genius in your own life and with others.

When you make this commitment to yourself, the informed guidance originating from the deepest source possible gives you a new baseline from which to reset your life goals. Fueled by your Innate Genius, you will now show up differently. Instead of trying to fulfill other people's expectations or follow road maps based on assumptions about how you should journey through life, you rediscover your true path. This road leads to the fulfillment of your authentic longing. You can be fully who you are destined to be.

Now, with imagination at the center of your life, you are ready to use your Imaginal Intelligence and your Innate Genius to contribute to the world and to meet its challenges and opportunities with passion and potency. In uncovering your Innate Genius, you find the necessary talents for today's world, for the times to come, and for the next evolution of the possible. "We all have the extraordinary coded within us," said Jean Houston, "waiting to be released."[6]

Part 2

In the World

Chapter 7

Utilizing the Imagination Matrix System

The resources available in the Imagination Matrix seed new ideation, creativity, and innovation. More than a theoretical idea, the Imagination Matrix is a fertile medium for problem-solving and a potent incubator of new solutions. In a world that requires innovation, it is imperative to have a process to reimagine old structures in new ways to meet the challenges of today and tomorrow.

The Imagination Matrix System transforms the elements of the Four Quadrants so they can be optimized and applied. This methodology combines cutting-edge research and breakthrough applications from the fields of earth sciences, depth psychology, new technology, and cosmology.

I have used the Imagination Matrix System in companies to facilitate creativity; in educational institutions to increase best practices of teaching and learning; and in government to provide blueprints for city planning and environmental stewardship. I have also utilized it with individuals to enhance personal growth and development. In working with this system, I have seen transformations, large and small, that have impacted individuals and institutions in powerful ways. The more adept you become at operationalizing the Imagination Matrix system, the more easily you will innovate and navigate through the personal, institutional, and vocational challenges you face.

You cannot access the Imagination Matrix System through rational thinking alone. It requires the move from the rational mind to the Curious Mind. Learning to open your Curious Mind formed the foundation of your inner work in part 1 of this book. It is the same in part 2 as well. Remember that to move from the rational mind to the Curious Mind, you must begin by putting a stop to your habitual mental processes of problem-solving and overthinking. Activation begins with a shift in perspective. Take some deep breaths, clear your mind, and become present to the here and now.

Activating the Curious Mind: The Quick Shift Protocol

Change context to change content. It takes a physical shift to make a mental one. Depending on your circumstances, walk on the grass; listen to the wind; take a mountain hike; or turn off the lights, take off your shoes, and feel what is beneath your feet.

Notice. What surprised you? Was there a sensation, an image, a feeling that moved or delighted you?

Focus on the new. If you are in a group setting, share this experience with another person. If you are alone, draw the images that came up or write them down. These actions concretize the experience of the new.

Awaken curiosity. Allow yourself to feel the wonder of new experiences through all your senses. This interplay awakens your curiosity. Now, you are ready to activate the Imagination Matrix System.

The Imagination Matrix System

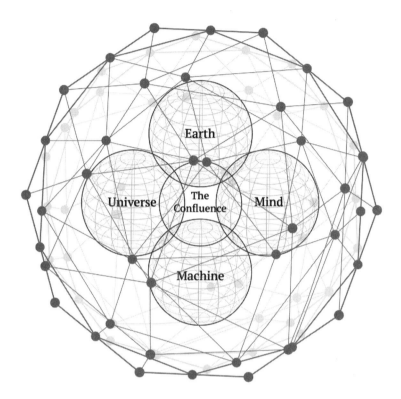

The Imagination Matrix System operates through a methodology, a template containing a series of steps that when performed in sequence result in information that is useful in a wide variety of areas, from the personal to the professional. It always begins with asking foundational questions through the lenses of each of the Four Quadrants. Then it moves to receiving the insights evoked by those questions. This is called *Quadrant Work*. When the Four Quadrants are activated in Confluence, a breakthrough occurs that is often unexpected, always exciting.

To illustrate the real-world functionality of the Imagination Matrix System, here I offer three scenarios that reveal how the system can be applied. Each uses the three phases of the Imagination Matrix System:

asking orienting questions, receiving insights from the Four Quadrants, and actualizing the new possible. You can apply this method to most any challenge for which you seek significant resolution.

Scenario 1: Optimizing Innovation in the Modern Workplace

I have introduced the methodology of the Imagination Matrix System to more than a dozen companies. The model functions well because it can be customized to bring the realms of deep imagination to the workplace and used to build toward unique outcomes for each individual company. For many corporations and institutions, particularly in the tech sector, employees are accustomed to working in shared, hive-like open cubicle spaces. Screens of all kinds are ubiquitous; there are few personal items on the desks and often no potted plants or pictures on the walls. In these spaces, creatives are asked to collaborate on projects—yet they remain focused on their individual screens, for the most part. Despite being in the hive, they often feel alone. Even when working from a distance, the home or office workplace often takes on many of these same characteristics.

For many, the pace is intense and overwhelming. It is not unusual to put in multiple sixty-plus-hour weeks in a row. Sprints consisting of uninterrupted attention on a single project occur regularly. Employees are driven by the aspiration that the products they help create will impact human experience in profound ways and define the future. Yet many feel an emptiness; something is missing in their day-to-day experience. I was challenged to use the Imagination Matrix System to inspire both the employees and the product-development process to the next level.

Quadrant Work: Asking Orienting Questions

Earth. If the landscape of the workplace could tell a story, what tale would it tell? What environments in your workplace are warm and inclusive? Cold and isolating? (These questions originate from deep ecology's teachings on nature's genius.)

Mind. What images, visions, or common narratives come forward? (This originates from depth psychology's insights into the Imaginal dimension.)

Machine. What is most helpful and what is most challenging about the various technologies that you are currently using or creating? (This inquiry originates from the innovation and functionality of new technologies.)

Universe. What image comes forward when you think of the ingenuity of famous inventors throughout history or previous leaders, elders, or founders in your industry? (This awareness originates from the vision passed forward from elders and the valuing of lineage.)

Quadrant Work: Receiving Insights

Earth. In the modern workplace, work stations within a building connect to networked work spaces in the home. This configuration parallels the interconnected systems of bees, ants, termites, and other beings found in the Earth Quadrant. Employees in these work-related hives, as with the instinctual intelligence of animals in nature-based hives, connect with the network for protection, cooperation, and transmission of information. The dynamic of a hive offers many opportunities. As isolated individuals, it's often hard for us to find the needed support and infrastructure to innovate. But as part of an interconnected hive, we enjoy the collective capacity to thrive and to adapt to an emergent possibility.

Mind. In the workplace, stories generated from the Mind Quadrant connect people both to imagination and to one another. When people feel the support and warmth of collegial relationships, creativity expands. Companies tell stories about their brand, products, and philosophies. These stories not only attract customers but can create a common narrative around values and purpose that becomes a source of motivation and pride for the labor force. When management encourages workers to share personal stories, imagination is awakened and supported. In addition, individual employees can stand out from the buzz of the hive and see their contributions acknowledged. This shared storytelling deepens comradery, promotes creativity, and increases the vitality needed for innovation.

Machine. The very technology that threatens to replace humans can also awaken the next evolution of consciousness. From the Machine Quadrant, the right use of technology opens generative ways of being connected never before imagined possible. Human imagination is companioned, stimulated, and perhaps enhanced through interaction with highly astute, empathetic robots utilizing shape-shifting visuals through programs like StarGAN v2, which use an AI neural network to generate new images by pulling from user-created networks.[1] Advanced technological systems like DALL·E allow innovators ranging from artists and creative directors to authors and architects to share their creations and feedback in networked workplace environments.[2] Innovation and creativity are assisted by the very technologies that were incubated and then constructed through the realms of deep imagination. We are yet to imagine the next iteration of technology, as it is always evolving.

Universe. From the Universe Quadrant comes the wisdom of keeping grounded while forever reaching for the transcendent. Each member of the company has a front-row seat to the limitless possibilities of the Imagination Matrix extending beyond the human generated. Human consciousness can be expanded to include the intelligence of the others with whom we share the planet. This shift opens new perspectives, fuels creative vitality, and enhances the capacity to imagine into the future.

Attaining Confluence: Integrating the New Possible

After the company utilized the Imagination Matrix system, the experiences of employees, vendors, and customers have undergone a quantum shift. The conformity engendered by open-space sterile workstations is gone, and the ecological imagination has made its presence known. Plants fill the space from floor to ceiling with fragrance, even though most employees work from home offices. Employees who choose to come into the office now can individualize their work spaces with personally inspiring items. To keep everyone rooted together and grounded in the natural world, each person is encouraged to add something from nature to their work space, no matter where their screens are located. One feels a deep sense of interconnectedness, as in a grove of trees.

Employees enjoy an increased feeling of belonging to something more: a place where innovation originates, is made visible, and is cultivated. Each employee, from founding CEO to the leadership team to line staff, now has something very personal placed around them, from pictures to artwork to altars that contain remembrances of elders, ancestors, and mentors—reminders of who inspired or supported their cutting-edge work in the first place. Their presence lessens the experience of isolation and motivates the next innovative breakthroughs.

Utilizing new developments in virtual reality, augmented reality, and mirrored reality, working teams are able to interact with one another in a variety of ways. They can assemble virtually and interact from anywhere in the world, including at the actual location of their project. Using new evolutions of mixed reality, their virtual working experience is personal, relational, right placed, present, and even sensate. When including the genius of new discoveries in technology, the work has become generative and innovative and interpersonally embodied in ways never before possible.

Their conversations with one another are no longer only about work products; they also tell stories of new discoveries. Joined together through technology, they interact with each other from their own individual office spaces. Now, each person contributes their Innate Genius to the collective. They are connected to one another and to the joint vision that brought each of them to this workplace. In these ways they forge the next true innovations.

Silicon Valley

I was invited to consult in Silicon Valley with the leadership team of a marketing company that was well-known for their award-winning work. The company managers believed that their team was stale, stuck, and burned out. My first meeting started off slowly; many people seemed obviously annoyed to take time out of their busy day. We began with the Quick Shift Protocol to activate the Curious Mind and the process of accessing the Imagination Matrix System. It was when the head of the design department raised her hand to speak that the floodgates opened. Instead of talking about future planning, as expected, what she brought to the group was shockingly personal. "I feel alone and isolated at this company and in my life. What can I do?"

The room was silent. Sharing at this level was new and unfamiliar in this setting. Then something rather extraordinary happened: almost half of those present raised their hands. Each person wanted to explore painful personal issues that they were struggling with alone. What emerged that afternoon was a revelation about what fuels creativity.

It came as a surprise to those assembled that it was not the study of data, consumer insights, and clicks that propels creativity. Rather, it is the transmuted psychic energy channeled from personal pain. The pain can be anything from isolating depression or relational breakdown to crippling anxiety. The raw psychic libido of essential human experience links to the force of timeless, universal stories. From sadness come essential stories of grief; from disappointment appear stories of failure; and from desire manifests the yearning for home. The impact of such archetypal stories is powerful.

The process of transmuting highly charged and maybe what might even be considered dysfunctional personal patterns into story sparks the generative energy needed for creativity. Once you peel away the layers of the rational mind and reconnect with the Curious Mind, the Imagination Matrix System can be utilized. Later in the meeting, the head of the design department continued to reveal more of her story. She admitted that she worked all the time. She was in constant adrenaline mode; she could not turn it off. It surprised her that in sharing this agitation with her coworkers, she had a flashback of the joy she had as a child when she sketched and created images. To help her activate her Curious Mind, I suggested that she create a new campaign without her computer, using colored pencils and pastels on paper instead. She could make a new story from what emerged that she could then share with her coworkers. Immediately, she began to relax. Just the hint of reconnecting to the source code of her creative process and the ideas that would flow from that pushed the pause button on her crippling anxiety.

In the case of the marketing company, this process that started with management eventually reinvigorated all the employees, including the leadership. Months later, they reported that the team was approaching their work with renewed energy, creativity, and personal passion to move the business forward.

Scenario 2: Reimagining Planning for Educational Institutions

In today's rapidly changing world, education institutions are finding it more necessary than ever to be nimble and responsive to the challenges of modern times. They are being called to reimagine curricular offerings and to embrace new technologies in creative ways. Institutions, many still in the mindset of nineteenth-century educational philosophies, need to fast-forward to the concerns of the twenty-first century.

Employing the tools of the Imagination Matrix System in an educational setting brings new perspectives and concrete applications. The essential challenges of how a school or university can plan for the staffing, the infrastructure, even the campus of the future are effectively addressed when using the Imagination Matrix System. What would the educational setting of the future look like?

Quadrant Work: Asking Orienting Questions

Earth. Are there stories that come forward from the land on which the campus is situated? In what ways are these stories incorporated into the mission/vision/aspirations of the institution? (These questions orient around the conviction that there is spirit in place and there are teachings beyond the human made.)

Mind. What dreams and/or visions do students, alumni, and administration have for the institution? If the walls could talk, literally and Imaginally, what would they say? (These questions originate in the idea of a *living psyche*, expressed through both people and things.)

Machine. Does technology support and/or distract from the learning experience? Does distance learning enhance this institution's ability to teach its curriculum? (These questions are derived from the ever-present inquiry into the confluence of new technologies and contemporary education, the emerging visions of teaching and learning.)

Universe. Is the founding vision of the institution still being manifested now? How can this lineage be honored and incorporated into the culture of the institution to benefit the generations yet to arrive on campus? (These questions originate from valuing the eternal teachings of mentors past, present, and future.)

Quadrant Work: Receiving Insights

Earth. Ecological systems offer the deepest analogies for sustaining a generative campus life. Trees, flowers, rock formations on campus foster connection to the teachings of the natural world. Each speaks to a sense of place. They provide the foundation needed for students and faculty to feel grounded, particularly when their heads are in abstract ideas. Staying connected to the natural landscape is a reminder of the world that exists beyond the screens, particularly when machines of every kind are now inserted into virtually all aspects of the learning process.

Mind. Archetypal imagery and story invite curiosity and inquiry. The enlightened learning process is Illuminated through the generative teachings of diverse perspectives in all cultures and traditions. People long to be met in the place of story. The diverse stories learned and shared in the campus setting call to the best of human potential. They create the knowledge of the future.

Machine. Technology assists and extends teaching and learning. Through virtual networking that utilizes platforms offering augmented reality and reality simulation, students and faculty interact in learning environments that include both content and an actual embodied experience of the subject matter. Through new technologies, interactions with a historical site, a laboratory in another country, or a mentor halfway across the world come to life in the contemporary classroom. Multiple levels of teaching and learning take place in the immediacy of the present.

Universe. From the Universe Quadrant, the evolutionary spark of the institution becomes visible. The life force flowing through the veins of the organization powers a strong heartbeat for all to feel and follow. In planning for a generative future, the recollections of the multiple communities and cultures of the past animate the blueprints for the future.

Attaining Confluence: Integrating the New Possible

The university of the future holds an elevated vision for the administrative team, faculty leaders, and students alike. When walking on the campus, one can feel at a cellular level that the learning environment is alive. The environment is animated through an intentional integration of nature aligned with the topography. When possible, classes and meetings are held in these outside sanctuaries, grounding and revitalizing all who partake.

The academy is equipped with new technologies of many kinds, from virtual and augmented to mirrored reality. These revolutionary new platforms make distance learning an embodied experience. Students living in the inner city, in rural areas, in the Global South, or in any other country regardless of socioeconomic status attend the university either in person or through sophisticated simulcast delivery systems.

As experiential learning opens imagination and enlivens community life on campus, so too does an integration of ancestral teachings into campus life instill the desire to learn and dream. At on-campus gatherings, elders are remembered and honored. Looking backward into lineage opens perception and perspective. Participating in an extended intergenerational, international learning community fosters a deeper sense of belonging. Planning for the future becomes more than a regulatory task. The planning process is a service, fulfilling the destiny, the calling, originating in the soul of the institution. When the leadership of an institution utilizes the Imagination Matrix System, sparks of excitement replace feelings of obligation. The desire to learn and the courage to answer the call emerge.

A University in Los Angeles

The president of Westbrook University in Los Angeles, Dr. Jennifer Richardson, called me one day with urgency in her voice. She was tasked to lead a long-range planning committee to determine next steps to increase admissions and retention while decreasing withdrawals and leaves of absence. External events, including the COVID-19 pandemic and a financial downturn, were impacting the desirability of attending institutions of higher education. Dr. Richardson explained that the overall mood of faculty and administration was at a low point. She was concerned. At their quarterly meeting, after receiving a detailed report from the board's finance committee, Dr. Richardson was given the directive: Take action.

We met together alone first, without her team, to design the way in which she as a leader could approach this large-scale task. We worked on a plan that would foster a group immersion into the realms of deep imagination. We would follow this by utilizing the Imagination Matrix System as a tool to unleash fresh insights as to what was needed now and for the future. I could see her enthusiasm grow as she became aware of how to facilitate a new generative vision of what might be possible.

We spent a week discussing the resources she had available to her (support staff, board members, family, and friends). We then explored her inner resources (institutional experience, self-care practices, and Supportive Soul Companions). This part of the conversation was new to her, particularly in the context of her institutional work. Not surprisingly, the idea of Supportive Soul Companions was an alien concept. However, when the Curious Mind is set in motion, working in imagination follows more easily.

The day of the meeting arrived. Dr. Richardson greeted her group of top administrators, senior faculty, and two board members. She then requested that before getting into the tasks at hand, each person either close their eyes or, in whatever way worked for them, take a moment to go inward. She led with two questions: "In the beginning, what brought you here to Westbrook University?" and "What aspect of Westbrook's mission resonates with your personal values?"

She paused and allowed two minutes to pass. Then she said, "Now I would like you to think of an image that represents your original impulse to be here." People were both surprised and somewhat skeptical about this exercise. After all, they needed to get started on urgent work. Did they really have time to play games?

However, crisis and clear leadership often loosen the attachment to the familiar. Dr. Richardson, in her pleasant yet firm way, directed each person to share the image. What occurred then was out of the ordinary for a Tuesday morning in a strategic planning meeting. Imagination entered the room. Curiosity was not far behind. The field of experience shifted. Just twenty-five minutes into the first hour of the first meeting, the realms of deep imagination had been evoked. The board room was buzzing! Not only were the creative juices beginning to flow, but, in addition, it was as if guidance from outside the familiar was manifesting.

Now, Dr. Richardson rose from her chair and said, "I want to share a vision!" This was most out of character for this ordinarily disciplined academic. She went on: "I can see future students enriching their scholarship and opening their minds to new images and ideas by utilizing this same process we have just experienced. It came to me with a flash of insight and with such urgency. We need to act. Now." Propelled by her example, others around the table began to break forth with ideas. The more imagination is met by receptivity, the more innovative ideation follows. Thrilled by the response, Dr. Richardson whispered to me, echoing my own words, "It is as if we are listening to what the pull of the future is asking of higher education."

As new ideas continued to come forward, the work of developing a multileveled, integrated plan of action to meet the key objectives emerged. The considerable expertise that each person brought into the planning process from their diversity of backgrounds was being met with high regard by others. As Dr. Richardson and I brought curiosity and imagination into the proceedings, a cooperative, even enthused interactive dialogue emerged. Each person's contribution was met as a valuable thread to be woven into a multicolored tapestry that would make Westbrook unique.

This was the first of many meetings. The planning committee continued to employ the Imagination Matrix System to generate ideas. Follow-up meetings included student leaders and then alumni. Two and a half years have now passed since the planning committee met with me. Two fall admissions cycles have occurred. Westbrook is experiencing the highest enrollment in the history of the institution. Though this could be attributed to many factors, the most foundational is the change in culture there. With a remembrance of the core values, the creation of an animated curriculum, and inclusion of all stakeholders, excitement is in the air. To this day, elements of the Imagination Matrix System continue to be used at all levels of the school. The university is prospering.

Scenario 3: Navigating the Challenges of Personal Life

As you work with the Imagination Matrix System in a variety of settings, you will notice how, in turn, the process is working for you. Through this work, your curiosity is animated and expands. When applying the system to jump-start creativity in the workplace or in other organizational settings, you can also use it to address personal concerns. You can employ similar processes to spark your own self-actualization. Many times, I have utilized the Imagination Matrix System with clients who come to me in my private practice. The system has significantly helped to clear anxiety, treat depression, and aid in other treatment goals. Overall, the Imagination Matrix System assists in restoring well-being and connection to life purpose.

One of my clients had sought me out because he was grappling with a pressing question: "How can I realize my potential and be in healthy relationships when I am so gripped with anxiety and isolating depression?" I worked with him for two months, utilizing the three phases of the Imagination Matrix System: asking orienting questions, receiving insights from the Four Quadrants, and actualizing the new possible. You can apply this method to most any personal challenge for which you seek significant resolution.

Quadrant Work: Asking Orienting Questions

Earth. How can the solidity of Earth help to ground you and relieve suffering? Can the beauty of the natural world inspire your personal well-being? (This orientation is based on the idea that human actualization is part of a wider ecological consciousness.)

Mind. What do your dreams and fantasies reveal about your life's yearnings and purpose? How do you gain the courage to fully explore what these images have to tell you? (These questions originate from the depth psychological concept of soul making.)

Machine. How does interacting with machines/technologies assist and/or limit your capacities to navigate life's challenges? Is this cyber-interaction an antidote to loneliness? (These questions are rooted in the idea that functionality of both the machine made and the human made exist in an Imaginal field of interdependence.)

Universe. Does connecting to a larger cosmos enhance your curiosity and wonder? What transcendent ideas, concepts, or beliefs connect you to the larger perspective? (These questions originate in a cosmology existing beyond the limitations of an egocentric orientation.)

Quadrant Work: Receiving Insights

Earth. The natural world is once again the foundational starting place. Experience the creatures and landscapes as they tell their story and reveal your place in it. You remember that you are a participant inside a wider ecology, not separate from it. The rhythms and pulse of Gaia awaken your own body's breath and pulse. The animated landscape becomes a place that assists you in navigating the challenges of personal life.

Mind. Images offer insights that connect you to your deepest personal resources. They are the lifeline to your authentic life purpose. Dreams and visions may be difficult to understand because images are metaphorical, but they have something to tell you. The images that come through (whether beautiful or nightmarish) begin to awaken your own story. Animating your dream images offers you access to the healing powers of dreams.[3] Through the Imaginal processes you have practiced earlier in this book, you reconnect to your courage and the resonance of your life force.

Machine. As technology pulls humanity forward, you find unprecedented connection to people (and avatars) worldwide. In human-computer interaction, the machine brings presence to those who cannot be available in real life. Utilizing new applications of advanced technologies assists you in navigating the challenges of personal life and in finding alignment with your authentic calling.

Universe. Your Curious Mind now allows you to shift from a habituated person-centered perspective to an Imaginal awareness in which creativity replaces linear thinking. Your vision changes. It is as if you experience through your heart and body, not simply through your eyes and head. Here, you perceive the bigger picture, which gives you a greater ability to meet the challenges of personal life. You can readily open the portals of imagination to Illuminated Consciousness[4] and the connection to all that there is and all that's to come.

Attaining Confluence: Integrating the New Possible

Through the Imagination Matrix System, you have reconnected with your potential. It is charged by the energies of the rich ecosystem of the plants and creatures who share the earth beneath you and the air you breathe. Your senses are highly attuned as you participate fully in the living interconnected ecology. The potent life force of the natural world has brought you back to ground, to your homeplace, and to your embodied self. It has called forth your own Innate Genius, which is your unique gift and purpose in the world.

Now, as your attention increases and your perception deepens, you acknowledge the many Soul Companions within. Awakened, you experience what it is like to be resourced from inner life. Your relationships with family, friends, colleagues, and lovers both deepen and widen. Your curiosity and wonder increase. The teachings from the mythic underpinnings of situations, feelings, and behaviors reveal themselves to your emerging sensitivities. You see the beauty on the surface and the wisdom of the depths in all that you encounter. You feel moved to share this sense of interconnection with all around you.

New devices and advanced technologies enable you to develop your skills. As your Imaginal bandwidth rises, so, too, your capacities as a user of new technologies increase. This opens you to a more relational life. You begin to expand your reach well beyond just your local community.

As you evolve, you actualize your true calling. You become a citizen of the world. You have a deep sense of belonging. Secure in the authenticity of your being, you find the courage to greet your destiny. Remembering the lineage of your elders and ancestors, you offer your unique contribution into the wider culture. Navigating the challenges of your personal life becomes easy. You follow your curiosity instead of your reactive, habituated patterns. Most importantly, you experience life's journey not as a burden, but rather as grace.

Discovering Potential

I met Sheryl in a workshop I held called Journeying in Deep Imagination, which focused on using the Imagination Matrix System. Right after the first presentation, Sheryl's hand shot up, not with a question, but rather with a statement. "For the past fifteen years I've worked hard at building a successful career in the business world," she said. "But while my nose was in spreadsheets, my husband lived a more creative and spiritually attuned life. One day, I looked up and realized that because of my intense focus on work, I have missed out on most other more creative and enjoyable aspects of life. If possible, I would like to open the creative, even spiritual side of myself and enjoy those qualities of life with him." She added, "I'm pretty sure that I cannot find my way alone."

Feeling increasingly worried, at times frightened about her situation, Sheryl had turned to self-help books and blogs. She had tried formulistic interventions. She had found recipes for self-acceptance practices and successful parenting. Nothing helped. The old patterns, the critical inner voices persisted. The ghosts from the past continued to haunt her, now with increasing ferocity. As she condemned herself for the escalation of, in her words, "dysfunction," she became concerned, at times desperate. Something else was needed.

At the workshop, I offered many of the skills that you are now familiar with. We began with simple journaling about supportive figures in life. Sheryl wrote and doodled. She made a sketch of her beloved grandfather, who was always there for her with love and support, even when her mother was obsessively critical of almost everything she did growing up. Her mother remained critical of her as an adult. Sheryl did what children often do in experiences of continuous assault: she turned the critic from the outside into herself. This inner critic sits on the shoulder and impacts behavior in virtually all areas of life.[5]

I suggested that Sheryl give her inner critic—her tormentor—a name, a face, even a body. I encouraged her to sketch the figure, to put it outside of herself and onto the page. Sketching enabled her to begin moving away from feeling possessed from the inside. When she did this, she felt some distance.

Sheryl found that writing and sketching in her journal, free from her internal judgments, was liberating. She shared with me that this process was like taking a journey into places unknown without the need to produce outcomes for others. She felt more energized, not depleted. In my follow-up conversation with Sheryl a few weeks after the workshop, she described how she slowly began to put away her to-do list. Following an exercise offered in the workshop, each day she took a short walk outside, then returned for twenty minutes of writing and sketching in her journal about what she had experienced. With her Curious Mind opening, her imagination stimulated, and the feeling of support from the workshop, Sheryl began to record dreams and experiences that were dreamlike.

One day a vivid image appeared to her in a dream. It was a ranch house and barn with horses, surrounded by rolling green fields. She felt it called to her. In her fantasies she wanted to move there. When she shared her fascination and new desire with her husband, he responded first with disbelief, then with enthusiasm. Her idea seemed so out of character. "Yes," he said, thrilled to dream along with her. "Let's talk further." He quickly added, "Sure, I could imagine us living in a place like that!"

His support energized her to continue. She allowed herself to move more fully into the realm of deep imagination. She invited in the archetypal stories, the myths that aligned with moving to the country and having horses. When in relation to the presence and fluidity of the horse, Sheryl told me, her body, which had been hunched over the computer for years, extended upright from her toes to the top of her head. She breathed more deeply.

Sheryl was opening to her authentic self and her yearning for a more creative life. As her deep imagination awakened, she could envision as well a more spiritual life. She reflected on what it would be like to combine her considerable business acumen with her creativity and the hints of her emerging spirituality. Then, she got inspired. She began to imagine ways of being in service to her community. Now, Sheryl is spending her time moving toward that goal. She is excited and empowered and ready, as she says, to give voice to the rest of the story.

Never has it been more imperative to access the Imaginal capacities and transcendent powers that move within and without each of us. The Imagination Matrix System offers the functional means to answer the call. The Imagination Matrix System helps you to find viable solutions, creative visions, and innovative prototypes for the new possible. When accessed through the Confluence of the Four Quadrants, the system is powerful and effective. You can use the Imagination Matrix System to add profound enrichment to your own life and the lives of others. By accessing your Innate Genius, strengthening your Imaginal IQ, and applying the system, you can lead an Imagination-Centered Life. In the next chapter, you will explore practical ways to do so.

Chapter 8

Living the Imagination-Centered Life

Your journeys into the realms of deep imagination and your utilization of the Imagination Matrix System were all intended to bring you here to fulfill the highest aspiration: living an Imagination-Centered Life.

My day started like many others, with nothing out of the ordinary expected to happen. The first item on my to-do list was a business meeting in town. The route I would take was routine. Yet, this day, something else came forward. I felt myself pushed by an impulse to open my Curious Mind and follow my curiosity. As I drove, I allowed myself to navigate by directions derived from an inner GPS. Instead of turning right at the intersection as usual, I took a left turn. I then took another left, and then another. I was now following the signposts of imagination rather than the fixed landmarks of the familiar.

As I slowed down to take in the new vistas, my Curious Mind opened ever more widely. The landscapes with their multicolored cactus flowers and newly blossoming nasturtiums were beckoning. "Here we are," they announced. My breath deepened, and my vision expanded.

When I finally arrived at my meeting downtown, my Imaginal Intelligence was completely engaged. Not only did I accomplish the tasks at hand, but in addition, because I arrived already enlivened by the Imagination Matrix, the seminar became an extraordinary flow of ideas. I was at ease, enjoying the act of teaching that is my authentic purpose. The world of the ordinary and expected gave way to the emergent possible.

Actualizing Your Life Purpose

When you are living an Imagination-Centered Life, you are anchored in your soul's journey. The creativity and spontaneity that you were endowed with from the beginning reemerges. As your relationship to the Imagination Matrix grows, a new clarity of purpose develops. The union between your everyday personhood and your inner self becomes more secure. You are grounded in your center place—the place of ease and well-being.

This rooting is referred to by some psychologists as "the primary anchoring system."[1] The anchoring system is imperative to the development of an actualized identity. Deepening your anchoring system creates the foundation for an abundant life and a sustained sense of well-being. In fact, there is no greater need in life than to find and develop the ability to ground into your life's purpose. Without foundational support from the inside, it is difficult to truly innovate or individuate. When feeling untethered from your purpose, you look to others for validation. When you rely on other people for direction, purpose, or meaning, you are always vulnerable to external judgments, agendas, and shortcomings. This exposure creates a secondary unnatural symbiosis, a dependency that is fragile by nature.[2] Of course, we all need and welcome the love and care of others. Yet when we are fully reliant on external resources at the expense of internal resources, trouble awaits.

It is no surprise that entire fields of intellectual pursuit orient to the study of interior life. Psychology brings focus to the wounding and healing inside. Virtually every therapeutic approach addresses this primary goal of connecting to the authentic self. From Abraham Maslow's hierarchy of needs to Sigmund Freud's psychoanalytic depiction of the personal unconscious, from object relations therapy to positive psychology, the strengthening of an inner nurturing relationship between the ego and deeper self is a core focus.[3] Guided by Samoan mythology, Karen Lupe has described this as "thinking with the heart."[4] Developmental psychologists often claim that the healthy nurturing needed for this inner development is dependent on unconditional love between a parent and a child.[5] Evolving a supportive inner parent who protects and cares for the vitality and curiosity of the inner child is, in one form or another, the goal of most psychotherapies. Though the methodologies differ, the primary message is uniform: bring attention and care to your inner life. Cultivating the skills of living an Imagination-Centered Life accomplishes this fundamental need.[6]

While I agree with these theories and have used them in my practice, I assert that a fundamental aspect of building a healthy primary anchoring system has not been taken fully into account. Journeying in the deep imagination is actually an essential contributor, along with all the other aspects of anchoring, to building a pathway to discovering your authentic purpose and to embodying a fully integrated life—or, as I call it, *Living an Imagination-Centered Life.*

Awakening to an Imagination-Centered Life

This process begins with you and you alone. When you are grounded in your center place, your mind begins to clear and to focus. Your purpose calls to you, and you are aligned with it physically, psychologically, and spiritually. When you are in alignment, you quite naturally stand on the foundation from which your Imagination-Centered Life is constructed. You take in only what resonates and discard the rest.

Awakening to an Imagination-Centered Life is about following your curiosity and wonder to your state of Illuminated Consciousness. You learned this in the Dig. Being in Illuminated Consciousness opens you to the knowledge and mysteries of an extended psychic field, to the abundance and vibrance of the Imaginal presence in all things Earth, Mind, Machine, and Universe. Illuminated Consciousness is first and foremost a reflective practice.

Illuminated Consciousness: The Quick Shift Protocol

Connect to your full body resonance. Deepen into the somatic experience of grounding to the earth.

Release your rational mind. Allow your Curious Mind to open to the Imaginal fields.

Attune to both the sounds and the silence. Let them embrace you in their infinite motion.

Perceive through multiple lenses. Bask in the *lumen naturae*, the light of nature, as the alchemists called it.

Yield to the experience of impermanence while still remaining connected to the radiance that is both within and without all things.

Owl Perception

When you are in the state of Illuminated Consciousness and aligned with your purpose, the beauty and magic alive in the people, creatures, places, and things of the world shine more brightly. You no longer live in a static world of fixed objects; rather, you reside, one among the many, in a fluid field of Imaginal waves that shimmer and dance. You feel the wisdom of the mountains and trees. People become keepers of stories that engage and excite you. Animals become guides and teachers. This ability to see all aspects of the worlds, above and below, is similar in some ways to the expanded perception of an owl.

The owl is both an actual bird with acute, specialized abilities and, too, a figure of human imagination. The owl's eyes are large. The forward-facing eyes give the owl its wise appearance as well as a wide range of binocular vision. The owl can see objects in three dimensions (height, width, and depth). Owls can turn their heads up to 270 degrees to the left or right and almost upside down. For owls, hearing is as important as vision. An owl's hearing is ten times more sensitive than humans', and it can hear sounds ten miles away. With their expanded vision (eyes that can see in the dark) and acute hearing (ears that can pick up the faintest of sounds), it is no wonder that the owl is thought to have mystical and supernatural abilities. The archetypal attributes of the owl—a wisdom guide, propelled by an inner light—models new ways of being conscious in the world. When you are in the state of Illuminated Consciousness, connected to the multiplicity, it is akin to experiencing the perception of an owl.

Living an Imagination-Centered Life: Tools, Skills, Applications

Utilizing the expansive point of view of the owl, you will be able to apply your Illuminated Consciousness to all aspects of your life. This includes your chosen or biological family, your love relationships, your profession, your workplace, and giving back to the larger community. Elevating each of these areas contributes to the overall richness of your Imagination-Centered Life.

Home and Hearth: The Place of Origin

Your home and the relationships between household members are of the utmost consequence to building an environment that supports your Imagination-Centered Life. The system dynamics in the home setting energize or dim the abilities of each of the family members. Not surprisingly, there is no "ideal" family. But when you envision your personal or extended family system as a primary container for imagination and the home as the place of soul making, then life in the family takes on a powerful new meaning.

The push-pull of the family constellation is often the very medium that vitalizes imagination. I'm not referring to pathological behaviors in a family, which might need to be addressed in a professional or therapeutic setting. But rather, in the ongoing dynamic of family life, there are opportunities to use the resources of imagination to transmute aggressive outbursts into constructive, even creative, expressions.

For example, a child or adult may seek refuge by withdrawing from the fray into the realm of the imagination as a response to distressed family-system dynamics. With doors shut, the bedroom, backyard, or office may become a sanctuary where the retreat into imagination creates space and protection. With eyes shut, you might find that the realms of active imagination become an inner sanctum where the imaginative process brings refuge and meaning. The imagination offers a channel for perspective and healing.

In my work with families, we have reframed and renamed the typical parental "time-out" as "time to dive in." Creating a separate and safe retreat place allows each family member the space to reconnect with their own center place instead of continuing to enact the family drama. Another tool I have used in my practice is to ask families to step back from the conflict and remember that your family is more than your immediate constellation. It extends backwards to include all of your ancestors.

Many cultures around the world include the remembrance of ancestors and elders in conversation to honor the value and stories of those beloved and who had come before.

For example, rituals of remembrance like el Día de Muertos, the Day of the Dead, which originated in Mexico, honor those who have passed. Other observances and rituals like All Hallows' Eve, All Saints' Day, and All Souls' Day also evoke the imagination and acknowledge the presence of ancestors in similar ways.[7] Rituals can take on a humorous tone when family members remember funny events and anecdotes about dead relatives and friends whose spirits come alive in the festivities. These rites often include the building of home altars with favorite foods and beverages of the departed placed alongside poems and lighthearted verses. Imagination is opened as the invisible souls of the now dead become present as members of the ever-increasing extended family.

As you have experienced, including an uncle, aunt, great-grandfather, or grandmother in your daily Imaginal practice offers a way to bring an additional sense of family connection to home and hearth. Your kin are the life force that fuses your soul's bloodline. These persons of the past now become present in your ever-deepening and -widening Imagination-Centered Life.

Family life, for better or worse, is our place of origin. It can be the place of wounding or the place of sanctuary. As you work with the Imaginal realms for your own healthy primary anchoring system, you can bring that health and wholeness back to your loved ones. That includes sustaining love relationships between primary partners.

This happened for Mel. She was stuck in a repeating cycle of shaming and blaming her mother. Each time a situation created a flashpoint between them, she would at once pull out her well-worn version of her family script: "This is not about me, this is your fault." From there the conversation quickly escalated to the all-too-familiar mode of listing all the gotchas, such as "I'm not the one who doesn't keep our house in order" and "When was the last time you took responsibility for anything?"

As I worked with Mel, we began to shift her focus away from what her mother was doing wrong and back to connecting with the Imagination Matrix System. She remembered that her Innate Genius called her to be a writer. As she opened her Curious Mind to this idea, she was able to begin changing the negative script that was derailing a precious relationship. Before responding to her mother, she now practiced pausing and experiencing herself in a bigger story, even imagining being the author and the receiver of creative dialogue. She began framing her assertive statements as wishes, not judgments: "Let's imagine ways of being together without fighting" rather than "You just don't understand me." Now, more than a year later, Mel and her mother are relating more harmoniously with each other. Reaching into the imagination for resources allowed Mel to find new possibilities for her and her mother to coexist in an Imagination-Centered Life. Mel is also writing her first novel.

Love Relationships: Honoring Your Partner

Marriage or partner relationships can take many forms. The union between two people differs in form and meaning from culture to culture as well as from couple to couple. People form relationship bonds for a variety of reasons, including legal, social, libidinal, emotional, financial, and religious purposes. Becoming married may be influenced by gender, socially determined rules, outside forces, and/or individual desires. The partnership between people is as unique and complex, as beautiful and challenging, as the persons involved. Yet behind the construction of partnership, one dynamic element is universally just so. Your relationship creates a vessel for the potential quickening of the imagination. Even when the energy of a union grows dormant at different times, the imagination behind the routine is forever present.

You may be surprised to learn that your relationship has more partners in it than those who are visible. Like the Imaginal figures you have discovered in your individual journeys, Imaginal presences inhabit the psychoactive field between you and your partner. As these invisibles of imagination become visible, the opportunity of living an Imagination-Centered Life as a couple awakens.

Of course, relationships are complex. And too, many times, they are deeply rewarding. They can also present some of the most painful challenges. Sustaining the love that brought you together with your partner is a yearning well worth tending. Dreams and imagination can offer support and assistance by giving you a way to also tend to what the poets name "the third body." This invisible lover is elusive to the touch, yet always present just behind the veil. The habitual routines developed over years can dim the bright pulse of this third presence, but activating the imagination awakens the vitality of this other, key partner in your relationship.

In your marriage or partnership, be on the lookout for the emergence of this Imaginal Soul Companion of your relationship. There are many kinds of relationships and configurations of relationships, and this teaching can be applied accordingly. It has been referred to in many ways across cultures. For some, it is the guardian angel of a relationship; for others it is personified as a mythic entity. This Imaginal presence has a force and a character that exists between you and your partner. In fact, this entity might have been partially responsible for bringing you together in the first place. It is the third body of your relationship.[8]

Getting to know this Imaginal presence opens your marriage or relationship to something more than the personal, where conflicts like power struggles, communication breakdowns, and unmet expectations are too easily constellated. Many of these dynamics are leftovers from dysfunctional patterns developed early in life and not just a result of your being together. When the marriage conversation occurs only in the realm of individual personalities, unmet expectations are too easily repeated. When you and your partner bring attention to the third body, you can rediscover what exists uniquely between you. In this way, you support each other in living an Imagination-Centered Life, individually and together.

Inviting the Third Body into Your Relationships

Honor your relationship by inviting the third body into the hearth of your Imagination-Centered Life. With your curiosity open, journey into your imagination and find the image of this Soul Companion, the third body.

Make it physical. As the Soul Companion becomes visible in imagination, give it physical form. Make a sketch of what you see or feel that works for you. Find a physical object that in some way depicts its essence, such as a stone or a flower.

Share this object with each other. Bring this symbol of the Soul Companion of your relationship with you as you go on hikes, vacations, or other adventures together.

Make an offering. Together, offer the object representing the Soul Companion a gift, as you would to each other.

Welcome in. As you care for the Soul Companion in your relationship, notice how it in turn cares for you. Take the time to share your experiences of what has occurred inside of you and what is happening between you.

As your heartfelt imagination awakens, Eros, the invisible lover, becomes present. Your life together deepens more fully and intimately. Robert Bly said it best in his poem "The Third Body":[9]

A man and a woman sit near each other, and they do not long
at this moment to be older, or younger, or born
in any other nation, or any other time, or any other place.
They are content to be where they are, talking or not talking.
Their breaths together feed someone whom we do not know.
The man sees the way his fingers move;
he sees her hands close around a book she hands to him.
They obey a third body that they share in common.
They have promised to love that body.
Age may come; parting may come; death will come!
A man and a woman sit near each other;
as they breathe they feed someone we do not know,
someone we know of, whom we have never seen.

Professional Life and Workplace: More Than the Daily Grind

Most of us spend eight, sometimes ten or more, hours a day at our jobs. Professional life provides the opportunity to manifest goals informed by your relationship with imagination. At the workplace, online or on-site, participating in a culture infused by an Imagination-Centered Life can offer meaning and fulfillment.

It begins with a reframe, a paradigm shift. Instead of asking yourself, *What should I be doing professionally?* or *What do others expect me to do?* you ask, *What are the figures of imagination asking of me, what is their desire?* In responding to these imagination-centered questions, you can then set goals and create professional meaning. Your Soul Companions are your new associates in a consulting firm of inner partners. As in organizational team building, it is not a matter of "I" but rather of "we." Your Imaginal LLC consists of many inner colleagues and partners. Planning sessions, board meetings, even conference calls first take place in the chambers of your inner life, well before you make outcomes explicit. In these assemblies of imagination, you hold discussions, vet various points of view, and conduct creative brainstorming sessions. You give each Soul Companion room to speak their piece, even when they are contrary. In these team meetings, you generate professional goals and incubate new directions for the future. A wise old saying goes, "Vision comes first, coin will follow." When you are empowered by the creative expertise of your Imaginal collaborators, prosperity can manifest on many levels. Professional success results from the enactment of your consultation with the Imagination Matrix System.

Turning to imagination as a primary resource has become attractive to major companies and graduate schools of business. Tech conglomerates like Apple and learning institutions such as Harvard Business School are now emphasizing curricula, training, and support in enhancing imagination.[10] These organizations realize that imagination is an essential tool for unleashing creativity and productivity. In a constantly changing marketplace, imagining what a company can *become* is as important, if not more so, than managing what has *been*.

As you have been learning, with imagination comes an increase in innovation and ingenuity. These traits are integral in expanding what I call the *Imaginal Bottom Line*. As important as the profit margin is in professional life, there is a need for something more, not separate from but in addition to profits realized from a successful business plan. As your professional life roots more deeply in the generative forces of imagination, an enhanced quality of life is a profit of another making.

Monica walked through life feeling above it all. In her mind, nobody could do things as well as she could. At the workplace, colleagues found her aloof and with an aura of superiority, and invitations to join them in gatherings were few and far between. Because of this, Monica felt increasingly alone. She came to one of my workshops. We started working with her dreams as a portal to the Imagination Matrix. Each morning Monica would record her dreams. Of course, it did not take long for her to discover the multiple characters and diverse landscapes that presented in her dream life were anything but superior.

As the dreaming psyche often does, it compensates for awake life circumstances. The superiority complex is often just the other side of the feeling of inferiority. As Monica endured the appearance of dream images that were wounded, deflated, or impotent, something new started to appear. In time and with support, her repulsion gave way to curiosity. As she befriended a few of her wounded dream images, she learned of their vulnerability—and, in turn, of her own.

Monica discovered that imperfections offered lessons to be learned. In her life, she began to shift away from her habituated reaction of "I can do it better than my colleagues" and instead to listen to the choir of voices saying, "We all have something valuable to contribute." In dropping into her Imaginal Intelligence, Monica found her outward behavior changing. She became more tolerant of others. At times, she even became fascinated with the unique differences, approaches, and appearances of coworkers she encountered. As Monica began living an Imagination-Centered Life, her life became richer and more interactive. Now she is more at ease at work. Her change in attitude and increased creativity have been noticed by senior management. She has been asked to participate in an advance planning committee, which gives her fresh opportunities to grow as a cooperative member of the company team.

When you engage in self-nurturing processes of working with the Imagination Matrix, a new quality of well-being manifests, giving rise to your innate creativity, which has been there all along. Being in your workplace with a sense of abundance opens you to gifting rather than hoarding. Older modes of energy depletion give way to the restorative powers of creation. It is important to sustain your connection to the realms of deep imagination and your Illuminated Consciousness to strengthen your creative capacities in the professional sphere.

⊗ Foundational Template: Incubating Creativity in the Workplace

An easy praxis for incubating and sustaining your creativity in your professional life:

The Dig. Greet each day with an immersion into the realms of deep imagination, your Dig practice. Even if you journey for only a short period of time, the rest of your working hours will be inspired by the morning's awakening.

On-screen journal. For those who work on computers during the day, keep a separate window open on your computer to use as your on-screen journal. Sparks from the Imagination Matrix often arise when least expected. Synchronicities occur. It can be an odd phrase in an email or text, or a bump into the unexpected while in a search mode. Don't pass these moments over as unnecessary interruptions that stop efficiency. Rather, note them in your on-screen journal. Over the course of a week, you will be surprised at how often imagination was present but you were overlooking it.

Review. Find a quiet moment to read through your on-screen journal. Give your curiosity some airtime. Notice what feels exciting. Giving space and place to the expressions of the Imagination Matrix infuses your workplace with Imaginal Intelligence just below the surface.

Dialogue. Find time to talk with colleagues, even if only online. Share what you have discovered from this exercise. It is in connection with others that curiosity is stimulated, creativity emerges, and relationships deepen.

Ensouled Stewardship

As the patterns in your life change, personally and professionally, a consolidation around your life purpose occurs. You replenish your confidence, extinguish your fear. Engaging life with confidence supports you to act on behalf of your core values ever more effectively. When you are in alignment with your purpose, your voice resonates with the assuredness of your convictions and vision. You offer to others a genuine expression of who you are in the world.

Now it is time to add to your Imagination-Centered Life the practice of serving the external community. I call this *Ensouled Stewardship*. Ensouled Stewardship differs from the belief that humans are solely responsible for the world and should take care of it and look after it. Or that through determination and willpower individuals should single-mindedly fix things. Rather, Ensouled Stewardship is a process of cocreation with others in its highest form.

In many faith traditions, stewardship involves the giving of time, talent, possessions, or wealth in the service of spiritual meaning.[11] The Maori social teaching principle of stewardship, *kaitiakitanga*, involves being responsible guardians.[12] In business and government, stewardship is an ethic that embodies the responsible planning and management of resources. The concepts of stewardship can be applied to nature, economics, health, property, information, and cultural resources.

Ensouled Stewardship is needed now more than ever. You might say this is truly a utopian vision that is blind to the realities of human nature. You would be correct in your assessment—unless something fundamental in the age-old patterning of human response can change. This change occurs when the Imagination Matrix is both included and valued as the bedrock of family life, relationships, the workplace, and the larger community. Previous modes of dominance and power are simply not bringing forth the innovation and imagination that we as a global community need to meet the consequential challenges threatening our well-being and sustainability. Ensouled Stewardship offers the generative alternative. Together, in the spirit of a more selfless service, you can become a guardian of what you hold dear—the beauty and vitality of a bountiful planet. Living an Imagination-Centered Life is nothing short of an answer to this call. Ensouled Stewardship is vital to the task of enhancing our humanity in a digital age and offers beauty, grace, and gratitude to all we hold dear.

Living an Imagination-Centered Life with an Illuminated Consciousness, you continuously connect to the Imagination Matrix. In the Confluence of the Four Quadrants, you can make wise use of the natural resources found there for healing the planet and for yourself.

Commitment to Yourself: Embodying Ensouled Stewardship

When you embrace Ensouled Stewardship as part of your Imagination-Centered Life, you not only fulfill your purpose but contribute to the well-being of others. You support the emergent possible. Your heart opens. Engaging in Ensouled Stewardship might take time. This process is meant to be practiced again and again. Start by setting an intention: "I will bring my Illuminated Consciousness to actualizing my practice of Ensouled Stewardship." Say it out loud. Choose a place where you can observe all that is around you, animate and inanimate. What is the world asking of you?

Notice. Use your owl perception to widen your perspective by viewing the multiplicity present in the people, landscapes, and things in and of the world.

Be present. Take the time to hear the whispers of the soul's yearnings coming from all forms of being—the nature-made, the human-made, and the machine-made.

Feel. The glimmerings of what you are called to do resonate through your body. Notice where they arise in your body and what they feel like.

Act. Repeat this praxis regularly. Doing so builds your capacity for sustaining an Illuminated Consciousness and your commitment to living an Imagination-Centered Life.

The informed guidance originating from the deepest source possible gives you a new baseline to reset your life goals. Instead of trying to fulfill other people's expectations or follow road maps based on assumptions about how you should journey through life, you rediscover your true path. This road leads to the fulfillment of your deepest longing. You can be who you are destined to be. Now, with imagination at the center of your life, you are ready to use your Imaginal Intelligence, your Innate Genius, and your Illuminated Consciousness to contribute to the world and to meet its challenges and opportunities with passion and potency. Again, these special abilities are necessary talents for today's world, for the times to come, and for the next evolution of the possible. So that, as Anneloes Smitsman has suggested, innate genius and "living systems network, embody, and actualize the quantum potentials of our Universe, which enable evolutionary capacities that make life possible and thrivable."[13]

Chapter 9

Imaginal Healing

The most intimate relationship you have in life is found not in the external world, but in the internal realms of your body. Every minute of every day you are linked to this primary homeplace in a union of deep belonging that begins at birth and continues to your last breath. This connection is not so much a mystery as it is a biological imperative. Your body is endowed with innate capacities of self-healing. The abilities for Imaginal Healing are sourced in the Imagination Matrix. When engaged, this internal somatic system turns on and establishes somatic resonance through your body. When Confluence is attained between elements of the Four Quadrants, the possibility for Imaginal Healing occurs. When your body/mind/function/spirit are not in alignment, you can experience a disconnection from the internal Imagination Matrix System. When this disconnection occurs, your body's innate healing processes become fragmented, and illness may manifest. Agitation and dysfunction, as well as corresponding emotional and psychological distress, may trigger physical affliction. When the Imagination Matrix System within your body is fully operationalized, the circulation of your energies flows more fluidly. When the intersections of body, mind, function, and spirit resonate in the Four Quadrants, your Imaginal Healing activates with additional potency.

Imaginal Healing is in part located deep inside the brain stem. When you evoke deep imagination, "signals travel up to the cortex and down through the neuro-endocrine system to affect the body at a micro-cellular level," according to Jungian psychoanalyst Robert Bosnak, founding director of the Santa Barbara Healing Sanctuary. "This activity, as natural and innate as the human heartbeat, has extraordinary therapeutic potential and is widely thought to trigger the body's own self-healing response."[1]

In addition, as you engage the embodied presence of your Supportive Soul Companions, their restorative rhythms and pulses steady your own. Now, you find a new Soul Companion, the Inner Physician, which presents itself when the healing process needs additional aid. Opening your Illuminated Consciousness, you discover this Soul Companion in your symptoms, dreams, and body sensations. The Inner Physician, when Illuminated, embraces you with a sense of deep caring and intimate support. You notice your body opening in both breath and ease of motion. Throughout human experience the wounded healer, the Soul Companion Inner Physician, has archetypal significance. This figure has the knowledge of the wound as well as the curative properties and medicinal treatments needed for the restoration of well-being.

❀ Soul Companion the Inner Physician: Four Steps for Illumination

Identify. Place your hands on the part of your body that holds your wound. Breathe deeply. Take some time; allow yourself to relax and your pulse to steady. Open your Curious Mind. Notice how your body responds in a healing way.

Name. Notice the Imaginal Healing process awakening from within. Use your Imaginal Intelligence to personify your body's self-healing response. Who is visiting now? Allow this figure to embody, come forward, and be known. Offer greetings to the Soul Companion the Inner Physician.

Acknowledge. Take time to host the visitation of the Inner Physician. Acknowledge that this Soul Companion has the homeopathic talent needed in the craft of Imaginal Healing.

Illuminate. Make an offering of appreciation. When you honor and care for the Inner Physician, its therapeutic powers magnify and surround you in their healing potential. Once you have Illuminated your Soul Companion the Inner Physician, include it as part of your ongoing team of Soul Companions and real-world caregivers.

Psyche and Soma

The idea that psyche (imagination) affects soma (body) and underpins wellness is both an old and a new concept. Recent discoveries in neuroscience validate healing traditions that are thousands of years old. Multiple cross-cultural studies demonstrate that the mind-body connection is indeed integral to healing and well-being.[2] My research into the effects of sustaining engagement with Imaginal Intelligence to promote well-being adds to these findings. As you learned previously, when we journey in the realms of deep imagination, adrenaline-driven alpha waves, which are sometimes related to stress, go down. Theta waves, often connected to body relaxation, go up.[3]

These findings point to new directions in how to treat disease and promote wellness. When today's medical procedures are assisted by the powers of the Imagination Matrix System, your healing experience is enhanced. In short, the curative powers within you mobilize, and your overall quality of life improves. In conjunction with your personal doctor and/or health care provider, who prescribe pharmaceutical medicines and treatment regimens, adjunctive Imaginal therapies can be of the highest value.

This happened with Julie. She was suffering from irritable bowel syndrome (IBS). When Julie came to see me, her life had become controlled and narrowed by both diet and travel restrictions. Eating anything slightly agitating to her digestive track triggered extreme diarrhea. Leaving the house created high anxiety, given the need to be constantly close to a bathroom. Julie was working with gifted and highly trained medical people. She was making some progress, but her condition persisted. She wanted to complement her medical care with something more.

To help Julie access her Imaginal Healing, I offered her the possibility of working with me and a team of other health care providers. On the team were a nutritionist, a bodywork practitioner, her physician, and an art therapist. After she was coached with the skills to cultivate and listen to her dreams, Julie had a breakthrough. In her dream, she saw her beloved dog walking in the backyard of her apartment complex. He seemed emaciated and ill. She could feel his suffering, which was very upsetting to her. My colleague guided Julie to relax, separate herself from her escalating worry, and open her vision more widely. She was asked, "Now, once again, go back to your dream. This time look at the entire backyard scene. What do you notice?" To Julie's surprise, she detected a new detail: her dog was slowly eating some of the grass. Doing so seemed to calm him down and make him happier. This grass appeared as a healing medicine. With the guidance of the nutritionist, for the next two weeks, before taking her regular medications, the team asked Julie to first spend time with her beloved dog, gently petting him and feeling his warm presence comfort her. Then, she would eat the calming equivalent of the backyard grass image in the dream. She imagined that the dream medicine of the grass corresponded to a rice cake with clover honey. Her team supported Julie in keeping her Curious Mind engaged, sustaining her bodywork, taking her medication, and tending ongoing dreams. After completing two weeks on this regimen, Julie reported that in feeling supported by this healing ritual, she had a sense of increased well-being. She was making significant progress in controlling her IBS. The activation and utilization of the Imagination Matrix System combined with good medical care offered a path for Julie to follow an integrative approach on her way to living a more fulfilling and healthy life.

Using the Imagination Matrix System to assist in healing physical illness rests on a long-standing premise that a person's psychological disposition affects their physiological condition. My belief is that in order to have any Imaginal Healing treatment work effectively, a person must evolve a positive relationship between soma, psyche, function, and spirit. Sonya Renee Taylor has affirmed the power of radical self-acceptance, self-love, and self-empathy as the crucible of healing self and systems, connecting body relationship and well-being, social justice, and transformation.[4] As many in the fields of depth psychology and somatic studies attest, the relationship between psyche and soma is central to beneficial healing outcomes. Research in both fields affirms this finding.[5]

When your Curious Mind is opened and the Imagination Matrix System is engaged, setting positive intentions for your Imaginal Healing triggers a somatic resonance and receptivity. As the neuroscience research in Imaginal Intelligence demonstrated, how and what one imagines affect moods, physicality, and overall well-being. Studies in what modern medicine describes as the placebo effect have demonstrated many times over that belief, anchored in imagination, supports, even creates, a healing response.[6]

Activating your Imaginal Healing powers begins with your capacity to change modes of perception. As you have learned, by putting on various lenses of perception, you are able to see through the literal experiences of awake life into the Imaginal depth that exists underneath. This talent becomes particularly useful when attending to physical illness. When you are not feeling well or are experiencing an acute wounding, changing your perception is of tremendous value. Your work is to see what psychic force or Imaginal figure lives under the manifest symptom of the disease syndrome. By seeing with an Imaginal eye, you can spot somatic disturbances.

The field of depth/archetypal psychology offers insight that is of tremendous value in this regard: behind the symptom is a habituated personality tendency, and behind this tendency is an image. It's good practice to make periodic scans of your physicality for images offering hints of disturbance. Of course, these hints do not necessarily mean that you are going to get sick. But often they do direct your focus to what is asking for attention on a somatic level. By changing your modes of perception, you can begin to glean what these images might be telling you.

⊛ Foundational Template: Opening Perception for Imaginal Healing

Your capacity to shift modes of perception is now familiar to you. In preparation for Imaginal Healing, it is time to bring increased precision to your praxis.

Owl perception. You can personify the abilities of the owl and use its mode of perception to scan your body for physical affliction. The owl serves as one of the many teachers modeling ways of extending vision and hearing. You have done this previously when utilizing your owl perception in your journey into the realms of deep imagination.

Imaginal X-ray. Reflect for a moment on what it would be like to visualize your illness, to see with heightened perception the intricacies of the image of your illness. In addition to the literal depiction of a sore throat or, for that matter, a virus cell, you see an Imaginal impression of the affliction. There are many ways to look at the various features of this picture. View it as you would an impressionistic painting. The image of the illness reveals something more. Notice what particularized designs come forward.

Awakening. Your imagination has joined the conversation. Your Curious Mind is awakened. The two of you, the observer and the observed, are in mutual regard. No longer do you feel identified, even possessed, by the illness; you are now in a relationship with it.

Perceiving differently. With your modes of perception widened, you perceive the restorative healing energies within the disruptive wounding incursion. As with the seemingly crippling forces of nature, you perceive the constructive energies that sustain the cycle of life. The rain brings water. The lightning offers fire. The winds are modes of transport. The same is true when envisioning your illness with wider perception. You now perceive the injury in a different way and can discover what inside the distress is life-affirming.

Utilizing the Imagination Matrix System for Imaginal Healing

The Imagination Matrix System offers an exciting new personal and integrative approach to the healing process. Now that your modes of perception are open, you can view the cause of distress and the potential for well-being through the insights provided by the Four Quadrants. Remember, the process always begins with Quadrant Work: asking orienting questions, then receiving insights. Then it moves to attaining Confluence: integrating the new possible.

Quadrant Work: Asking Orienting Questions

Earth. Physiologically, what is my affliction, and where does it manifest in my body?

Mind. Was there a wounding experience in my past that contributes to my physiological condition now?

Machine. Which organs or body systems are dysfunctional and how? What are the energetic obstructions within my affliction?

Universe. What belief system gives me access to the powers of positive healing intention?

Quadrant Work: Receiving Insights

Earth. The Earth Quadrant is the somatic ground from which your physical affliction manifests. From this ecosphere, you find the roots underpinning the physical illness. You discover the imbalance from which the wounding originates. And, too, you gain insight into the life-giving generativity sourced in the fertile soil of Earth. You access the procreative ground from which the healing process initiates blossoming new growth from the dry, sterile field of helplessness and fear. Through the process of the Dig, you excavate the Earth element embedded in the other side of your physical injury that brings Imaginal Healing and recovery.

Mind. The Mind Quadrant is where the Imaginal expression of your injured physiological condition presents itself. Through this quadrant, you can identify the psychological condition that contributes to the wounding. It is here, too, that you gain access to the curative psychoactive forces that inform mental intention, positive belief, and curative expectations. This is where you meet your Inner Physician and other Soul Companions who assist in your Imaginal Healing.

Machine. The Machine Quadrant is the place of discovering the functional obstruction that creates and, too, is caused by illness. In this quadrant, you discern the operational breakdown that is causing the stoppage. You also find the Machine's capacity for sparking and recirculating your life force. Here, you use your owl modes of perception to see through and around both the structural impediment and the psycho-emotional wound that creates the limitation in your body. In addition, you find what Imaginal capacities you need in order to release the healing vitality (life-affirming chi) of flow. This momentum ignites the curative somatic resonance needed for well-being.

Universe. The Universe Quadrant offers you the capacity and magic to discover the disconnection that has rendered you powerless and ill. You find the will to heal and the belief that you can do so. You utilize this power of positive intention for wholeness and well-being. From the cosmic source comes the knowledge to create the curative balm aligned for your Imaginal Healing journey.

Attaining Confluence: Integrating the New Possible

From each of the Four Quadrants, you gain the essential elements that are vital components of the Imaginal elixir: the healing Imaginal medicines. From Earth comes the regenerative element of fertile soil. From Mind, the psychoactive wind of positive intention. From Machine, the fire that energizes motion and mobility. From the Universe, the watery fluidity of the interconnected cosmos.

The Santa Barbara Healing Sanctuary, a center for integrative medicine that I cofounded, asked me to contribute my approach to connecting psyche and soma in conjunction with the Imagination Matrix System. At the healing sanctuary, therapists, artists, and somatic practitioners, along with top medical doctors and trained dream tenders, cooperate to support and attend to each patient's physical affliction. Emphasis is given to the centrality of healing dreams. Imaginal medicines assist in the practice of integrative medicine. By applying the Imagination Matrix System to access Imaginal medicine, we have helped many people find their way to Imaginal Healing and to better lives.

A Healing Journey

A woman named Rita, in her early forties, suffered rheumatoid arthritis in her left shoulder. The pain was so acute she could not raise her arm or sleep on her side.

Her family doctor referred her to a rheumatologist, who confirmed that degenerative arthritis had set in. The doctor prescribed anti-inflammatory medications to promote joint healing, as well as painkillers. However, her physical throbbing increased, and her feelings of helplessness grew. She was a mother of two young children, and as her condition worsened, she became more and more agitated and depressed. Rita sought out an additional treatment strategy, one that would offer a more holistic approach.

At the sanctuary, the integrative approach to Rita's illness included continued consultation with her medical doctor along with bodywork, expressive arts, anger management, healing baths, community support, and dream and Imaginal work. We led Rita through working with the quadrants of the Imagination Matrix System—Earth, Mind, Machine, and Universe—to develop the Imaginal medicine to be used for her healing work.

First, we asked her to name her affliction and to note how the illness was creating an imbalance in her life. She reported that "My energy is drained by the constant pain; my contact with others is restricted by the limited use of my arms. Even hugging is now difficult!" When she reflected on what she yearned to recover, we led her to imagine her mobility and life force in the context of the fertile soil of Earth's regenerative capacities.

Next, we asked Rita to consider the psychological condition that got constellated due to the continuing pain and suffering (from the Mind Quadrant). She was quick to tell of feeling a sense of helplessness that was accompanied by anxiety and fear. We led her to consider the energy source that creates anxiety and, too, the fire energy that *is* anxiety. She began to remember the "high energy self," as she called it, whom she had once been but was now buried. On the other side of the anxiety and fear existed the energy of determination. When we asked her to name this, she said, "This is my life force, my fortitude."

We then turned to the functional aspects (from the Machine Quadrant), asking her what functional blockage her arthritis was causing. She reported, "My shoulder is frozen, and I do not feel any circulation of energy in it." To that we inquired, "If your shoulder is frozen, what can you imagine would warm it and set it back into motion?" Our staff offered Rida an idea to consider: "If your determination acted like a warm lubricant, could you imagine applying it to your shoulder, which would return it to use, feeling like a well-oiled machine?"

Lastly, from the Universe Quadrant, we asked Rita to imagine what would offer positive intention and belief for her healing. In this way, she could imagine her body in connection with all the universal healing energies.

Now, it was time to attain Confluence, using the elements of the Four Quadrants to create the Imaginal medicine that she would integrate into her healing practices. We asked Rita to imagine placing all four Imaginal ingredients into a small chalice, represented by a physical bowl. First, Rita placed some of her life force as symbolized in the energy of Earth's fertile soil into the bowl. She spent a few minutes running her fingers through the nutrient-rich dirt to experience its generativity. Second, Rita made a sketch to personify her experience of determination. She began doodling with colored pencils; a red, gray, and purple column appeared, with an animated arrowhead at the top. Then, this "column of determination" became a figure with focused, purposeful eyes and strong arms and legs. We had Rita place the chalice containing the generative soil on top of the page with the picture.

Third, we asked Rita to rub her hands together with some vigor. We directed her to extend the functionality of her hands and fingers and generate the heat that got created by this rubbing of hands. She wrapped the chalice with her picture and placed her warmed hands around them to heat up what was being created. Fourth, we invited Rita to imagine strength and positive energies extending throughout her own body, touching into her muscles, nerves, and lungs. We offered her the concept of "holding the chalice of generative Earth, wrapped in the picture of energetic determination, heated by the warmth of your hands, which connects into all parts of your body."

Finally, we coached Rita on how to apply the Imaginal medicine to the muscles, tendons, and joints around her shoulder. Using positive intention and the expectation of significant healing, she placed the Earth-filled, picture-wrapped chalice on a bedside table in her bedroom. We encouraged Rita to experience this space when needed as her personal healing sanctuary. Rita was encouraged to recreate the heat between her hands, and to place her palms on the arthritic areas of her back, shoulders, and arms. In addition, each time she was going to take her medical doctor's prescribed medicines, she would first warm them up with her hands, infusing them with the healing energies of the Imaginal medicines before ingestion.

We advised Rita to follow this praxis in coordination with her medical doctor's prescription protocol. She quickly started to feel better. Six months later her fluidity had improved, and her pain had dissipated. She reported a feeling of renewed optimism and vitality: "I got my life back, and now I can give wholeheartedly to my creative work and to the people I love."

Accessing Imaginal Healing: The Quick Shift Protocol

You can do many things on your own to initiate Imaginal Healing by utilizing the Imagination Matrix System. There may be times when you do need further help from trained health care providers, but this quick practice can be useful as part of your ongoing self-care. Results may vary but most people report an improvement in vitality, resilience, and overall quality of life and well-being.

Begin your applied praxis by drawing a large square on a piece of paper and dividing it into four sections. In each section of the square, you will place a description of your wounding and your healing through the lenses of each of the Four Quadrants:

Earth. Ground yourself. Name your illness. Write this name in the top left box.

Mind. Identify the psycho-emotional components. Make a doodle of this feeling in the top right-hand box.

Machine. Describe the mechanical limitation you feel. Put these words into the bottom left box.

Universe. Name your positive intention and healing expectation. Write this in the bottom right box.

With your Curious Mind open, your chosen mode of perception engaged (owl perception, Imaginal X-ray), perceive the pattern that connects the Four Quadrants you've just articulated. Use the back of the paper as a space to write this down. By attaining Confluence, you create the Imaginal medicine that can aid in your healing.

Repeat: You can revisit this exercise as many times as needed.

Imaginal Healing

Imaginal Healing is designed to free your life force from the bounds of physical and psychic distress. It is not a cure-all for disease, but rather works in complement with other traditional health care practices and practitioners to assuage *dis-ease*. When you work with your Inner Physician and the internal healing energies begin to recirculate, the same thing happens in your physical body.

When you attain Confluence utilizing the Imagination Matrix System, your body responds in a curative way. Moving in concert with the rhythms of the Four Quadrants and the theta state inspired by deep imagination, somatic resonance releases self-healing capabilities. We are just at the gateway of discovering all the capacities of somatic movement. In the fields of medicine and healing, recent studies in neuroscience point to new directions in the ways we think about and treat disease and promote wellness.[7] Going forward, we will be able to treat the onset of illness in a restorative way and/or ongoing disease syndromes with renewed healing vitality.

Utilizing the Imagination Matrix System offers new opportunities for Imaginal Healing and increased well-being. It is this capacity to journey in the realms of deep imagination that improves your quality of life today and pulls humanity bravely into the future.

Chapter 10

Keeping Our Humanity in a Technological World

Is cyberspace taking over our human Imaginal space? The answer is: Yes—but not really, not fully. As machine-driven technology increases, so too must human consciousness evolve. Each functions via an operating system that is unique to their making. In the twenty-first century each needs and requires the intelligence (artificial and Imaginal) of the other to evolve. The digital platforms that you interact with are created through the Imaginal Intelligence of people interacting in creative design work. Keeping our humanity in a technological world requires both humans and machines to evolve in cocreative, collaborative ways.

Before we can go further, it is necessary to have a common definition of the word *humanity*. If we start with its Latin antecedent, *humanitas*, it is the idea of an essential human nature that is rooted in kindness and compassion, a heartfelt sympathy and consideration for others. I believe that the definition of humanity also incorporates self-love, sourced in the wisdom of your body and the intelligence of your emotions. In its most essential form, humanity is a relational concept. Sustaining your humanity is to remember and nurture your essential care for yourself and others.

To the extent that technology keeps you distant from your humanity, it can be viewed as pathological, splitting you off from the wellsprings of deep imagination. When perpetuated, this separation leads to states of depersonalization, isolation, crippling anxiety, depression, and even the manifestation of emotional and physical illness. However, the very ingenuity that went into creating the technology from the beginning offers the Imaginal Healing needed to prevent disharmony. Your relationship to the Imagination Matrix is what treats the alienation caused by the too-muchness of technology.

I believe it is the mindful interaction between technology and the people who use it that will allow humanity to move forward to a more elevated consciousness. With technology, you can deepen your human connections with others in ways that defy distance and span thousands of miles. You can communicate with people and communities that matter to you and find like-minded and like-hearted people with which to create intimate groups in which to share meaningful experiences. Currently, of course, there is a lack of embodied presence in the purely-screen connection with others. This is being addressed in the frontiers of virtual and augmented reality. The promise of these emerging collaborations is to deepen, not deaden, humanity. Any experience has the capacity to numb or to enliven curiosity and imagination. How might getting curious about technology's possibilities open portals to the deep imagination? The ultimate impact and new ideations of advanced technology are still unknown. Through accessible multisensory platforms of mixed realities and AI, your human expression could potentially be increased, and your full-bodied personal emotional responses are communicated. I believe this creative collaboration is the key to sustaining, then enhancing our humanity in a technological world. It is a cocreation based on mutual self-interests.

Machines need continual input to update their essential programming. At their core, they are dependent on the human imagination to create the next generations of new products. And, too, people need the assistance of machines to more abundantly sustain life—from diagnosis to treatment of illness, from navigation to communication, from conducting business to living in community. Let's not forget that machines exist because of human imagination, and humans survive and thrive through the assistance of machine intelligence. Humans need to sustain their humanness; machines need to become more attuned to and supportive of human interaction. When in appropriate balance, both experience the benefits of a procreative relationship. This balance for us can be found only in the interaction of the Four Quadrants; no one segment can be more controlling than the others.

When the Machine Quadrant and the technology of the modern world are out of balance with the other quadrants, you can feel separated, alienated from your center place. The way back to your humanity is to reopen your Curious Mind. Simply put, this is the shift away from the literal to the metaphorical. You shift from the quantitative activities of information gathering typified by machine intelligence to a qualitative sensitivity of aesthetic experiencing.

If we view the fate of humanity in a technological world aesthetically, we uncover something unexpected. As technologist and entrepreneur Rob Patrick has observed, "I came to realize that when we allow ourselves to see a thing from a new perspective, it is not the thing that changes—it is us, we are part of something larger."[1]

Experiencing the world through your Curious Mind widens your perception. The currents of imagination that fuse all creation, including your technologies, come increasingly into awareness. When perceiving aesthetically, not simply rationally, you sense the presence of psyche in the software. The algorithms that fuel technologies take on an archetypal sensibility. Their movement, their motion, can be viewed as being orchestrated by the programmers' code as well as having an Imaginal life of their own.

David, a software engineer who is a member of my Dream Tending and Imagination extended community, shared this idea:

> The algorithm is not a hardwired piece of machinery, nor is it a piece of software; it is the image of the patterning, the movement, the dance . . . which the hardware and the software are trying

to emulate. Whether the elements are cards, numbers in an array, cherished photos, or IP sockets, the algorithm speaks to their motion. The algorithm functions in archetypal ways, it is like an archetype, a psychoid phenomenon. As if there is a spark or fragment of an imaginative flow that is given a priori form within the hardware, in the software, and between the two.

In the times in my life where I have written software implementations of algorithms, I'd often close my eyes and imagine the movement of the elements, the dance of it, and from that living image, try to write instructions so that my software can participate in the dance. Drawing it out with little examples and lots of arrows of movement helps me distill this flow into steps; it is a kind of dance after all. Then I translate these steps into a language my computer can understand. In doing this, I am sharing something with the software, something imaginative, a little spark of psyche.[2]

Dreaming the World Forward

The answers of tomorrow are coming from children growing up today who have interacted with technology even at birth. The old paradigms have fallen away. These digital natives are the generators of the new cocreation. They experience everything, including technology, as having an Imaginal presence. Technologies when viewed as living images originate in the subjectivity beyond physical experience—they start in dreamtime, in Imaginal Play.

Traditional approaches to working with dreams and imagination view images as signs that literalize developmental or situational experiences in personal life. This point of view is not Imaginal. This domain of consideration is often referred to as the *personal psyche* or *personal unconscious* based on a linear history. The fields of depth psychology and mythology have developed additional approaches that view images as archetypal. In this mode, the field of experience refers to the *collective human psyche* or the *collective unconscious*.

I believe that the definition of *collective unconscious* needs to be extended to include technology. Technologies have a psyche of their own. They have a subjective interiority that presents itself in images. Young people are particularly vulnerable to these images, some of which reflect the world's suffering and can cause physical and psychological afflictions. In the frenetic pace of modern life, children need the help of adults to slow down. Adults also need to learn to slow down. When working with living images in both adult and children's dreams, I notice how they impact waking life. I have become increasingly aware that adults need to pay attention to their children's interior lives, as the relentless images produced by technology and the world's psyche can visit their dreams. Children and young adults can experience these images, sometimes nightmares, as personal, even though they are not of their own making. The darkness lingers in waking life and can impact the way they are imagining their future.

This happened with a young man who came to see me in great despair. The seventeen-year-old shared this dream:

> In the dream I see the entire planet. It is the size of a giant robotic head. It is like a mechanical seed. I notice that it is MY head—I am the Earth. My hands are outstretched, and I see that I hold all of the world's populations in the palms of my hands. A huge energy moves through me. I realize that I need to stay very still; if I even move a finger, just a little bit, hundreds or thousands of people will fall off and die. I use all the strength that I have not to move a muscle, not even a little bit. I stay as still as I possibly can. I must sacrifice my personal life and stay paralyzed so nobody else will fall off and get hurt. Wow. I think this is much bigger than I am. I realize I don't have a choice but to remain paralyzed. I must keep my balance to save the people. The only thing to do, the best thing to do, is to dedicate the rest of my life to staying completely still. I have no other choice.

We worked through his dream together. In tending a dream, I look to understand the living images. Here, it would seem at first that the boy's outstretched hands, holding all the world's people, is an embodied image of his sense of responsibility. However, it is not only about him personally. It is the world's dream telling its plight in the images of this boy's dream and asking for help. It hauntingly illustrates the point made by activist Dr. Helen Caldicott, who said, "It is as if the death of our planet is being grieved in the dreams of our children."[3]

Of course, some of what is pictured in the dream may be an expression of his personal condition. He may be suffering from anxiety, or isolation, or an inflated feeling of power or powerlessness. He may be experiencing the pressure of holding too much now. However, if we surmise that the world's fragility is expressing itself through dream images hosted by this young man, we can see something more. In addition to his personal circumstances, the dream may be telling of the dangers of an over-technologized world and the toll it is taking on our young people.

When working with this teenager, I suggested he look at the robotic head/seed more deeply. I invited him to breathe and feel the sensation that arose in his body. Then, I suggested that he look again. The head/seed became more embodied, more organic. Two things happened that offered both insight and relief. First, as the head took on life separate from the machine, so did he. Second, when he realized that in large part he was dreaming of the world's condition, not simply his own, he relaxed and felt relieved.

Dreams come to those who are open to receiving them. Our children are permeable to the dreams of a world that is in pain and asking for attention. For the most part, children's nightmares occur in the family home. Family life is a primary crucible where the possible, in addition to the painful, is present and can be acknowledged. To do so requires finding ways of affirming and nurturing the Machine Quadrant as an integral aspect of life, but not as a dominating force.

This is particularly important today, when in dreams and imagination the Monster in the Machine is omnipresent. Very young children are generally filled with excitement and wonder at playing with technology. But older children, and teens in particular, feel the presence of this Shadow Soul Companion as it moves through the collective psyche. You too may feel its presence when you experience an overload of tech. It is a sense that your life is ruled by the machine, which all too often is in fact true. When you have this realization and the monster is on the loose, you have the resources to change the predicted outcome of its threat.

When asked how to get out from under the oppression and possession of cyberaddiction, now at worldwide epidemic proportions, I suggest the simple steps below, which Follow Curiosity. Resourced by the realms of deep imagination, dreams come with hints of new possibilities. As you learned in practicing the art of Imaginal Healing in your wound, here, too, exists the necessary healing elements for well-being.

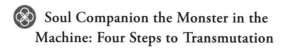

Soul Companion the Monster in the Machine: Four Steps to Transmutation

Observe the Shadow. Notice what first alerted you to the monster's presence. Was it your body (backaches from hunching over your laptop, wrist soreness from too much keyboard time, bleary eyes from screen light)? Or your moods (isolation from personal interactions, alienation from social gatherings, information overwhelm)?

Personify the Monster. Have some fun. Get some watercolors, brushes, and a big piece of poster paper. Remember what it felt like when you were a child and would uninhibitedly splash paint onto the paper, using your brushes or your hands? The idea is to go for it. Let the Monster in the Machine find expression by unleashing your body pain or emotional mood onto the paper. This is not a drawing assignment. It is also not a psychological exercise. You are expressing in free form the colors and shapes of the Monster in the Machine.

Name it. Now the monster is out of the closet. If a name comes forward, write it down.

The Monster Transmuted. If you feel open and safe doing so, hang the picture where you can see it. Also place your protective figures around it. Just as with other Shadow Soul Companions, now that you have Transmuted it, it takes on powers that offer positive guidance. The Monster in the Machine now has the ability to facilitate and animate your dreams, originality, and creativity.

Family Life Is Imaginal Life

Imagination is not static, not programmed. It is the creative presence that shapes how we humans, especially children, grow and develop. The family unit, chosen or biological, is the home place of our Imaginal life. A healthy family of today needs to work differently than it did ten years ago, thirty years ago. Cultivating a balanced relationship with technology in a home pervasive with technology begins by reimagining the family system to both include machines and build into the home environment ways that encourage family members to be off machines as well. Hands-on, screen-free activities—walks in nature, attending community theater, visiting the downtown, time at the museum, playing in the park, planting and tending a garden—nourish imagination. These are some easy-to-incorporate activities that allow family members to experience new ways of being in relationship with themselves and with one another. When children balance online time with interpersonal human and nature contact, a generative phenomenon becomes apparent. A new awareness evolves.

As family life opens to include and support journeying in the realms of deep imagination, the field of interpersonal relationships shifts. Family members notice and then welcome the Imaginal others who are active participants in the family's lives. These Imaginal figures originate in the psyches of family members and, too, in the ever-present home devices or those at school or a library. These Imaginal others are present at all hours of day and night and in all rooms of the home, including at the dinner table. They can be experienced as living images, like Soul Companions, or as machine created, like avatars.

In family life, the existence of online presences—avatars—presents both a challenge and an opportunity. Left unseen and unattended, their influence goes unnoticed. Family members have little awareness of what or who is contributing to moods, impressions, and values. On the other hand, when the Imaginal others are perceived and brought into relationship within family life, the opportunity to enhance conversation unfolds. Engaging these living images opens access to a wider field for conscious Imaginal play. Developing relationships with the Imaginal figures in family life goes a long way toward sustaining your humanity in a technological world.

Including Imaginal Figures and Avatars in Family Life

Family life today consists of more companions than ever before. Online identities, avatars, and personas evolved in virtual reality are as present as flesh-and-blood humans. Many family members spend multiple hours a day in cyberspace, and often their primary relationships are with figures in virtual reality rather than persons in the family. This is the environment that children of today grow up in: a field of consciousness populated by people from the virtual world.

This widened community including natural and virtual selves is not necessarily a bad thing. Once we recognize it as the new normal, it becomes possible for us to set a larger table, to invite both the human evolved and the virtual made into an ongoing family conversation. Children as well as adults use their computers as tools in school, the workplace, and at home to learn new things, communicate with others, and express their artistic ideation. Children grow up with their machines and with the multiple virtual identities they have created to make journeys in cyberspace. Similarly, adults have grown to rely upon machines to navigate the necessities of everyday living. Rather than exiling virtual figures and setting them against family members, it is better for us to embrace the existence of both in the household and find ways of developing constructive and rewarding relationships between the two.

Instead of shutting the door to a child's room or posting Do Not Disturb signs at the parents' work space, it is possible to find appropriate ways of inviting the many virtual selves into a wider family conversation. Creating a larger living room, as it were, and making set times for welcoming imaginal interaction between family members and the figures generated by technologies brings integration, not separation, to the family unit.

⊗ Foundational Template: Welcoming Imaginal Figures into the Family System

Prep. Set a half hour aside when your family can be without distractions. With art supplies nearby, invite members of the family, including the children and teenagers, into a conversation. Slow yourself down, evoke your Curious Mind, and open an attitude of listening without an agenda.

Share. Offer a story about one of your own Soul Companions or avatars. Start by saying, "This is who I've been thinking about recently." This gives other family members permission to share a story of their own.

Describe. Ask each family member about the characters/figures/avatars whom they are currently interacting with. Allow time and space for each to describe their online experiences. Be patient. Let the explanations unfold spontaneously.

Deepen. Open your Curious Mind and ask positive, open-ended questions (a "how," not a "why," question; not a yes or no question), allowing each family member to reveal their source of fascination. Without making judgment nor jumping into interpretation, listen to the importance each member's experience holds for them. Stay with your curiosity—there's no need to find an "answer."

Acknowledge. Offer a witnessing presence during the conversation, so your family members feel you acknowledge the place of the many selves in their virtual lives.

Invite. Give the characters or concepts alive in virtual reality a place in the expanded family experience. Schedule a follow-up time in which you will visit together to continue contact and conversation.

Repeat. Repeat this process to create an ongoing family dialogue.

The Grandchildren

Our eldest son asked my wife and me if we would watch their son and daughter, aged three and five, for an evening at their house. We knew we had an eventful night ahead of us. Dinner, play, boundary setting, rituals of bedtime, and unknown interactions awaited.

As is almost always the case, when we arrived the kids were happy to see us. Within moments they were jumping into our arms, and also asking, "Did you bring any presents?" We enjoyed a fulfilling dinner-time experience, and even the cleanup went well. Then, unexpectedly, there was quiet. I asked my wife, "Where did they go?" "In their room, I think," she responded. Sure enough, the kids were planted in front of a TV screen watching animated versions of Supergirl and Spider-Man. Both are high-production spectacles.

Quite literally entranced, neither child said a word in twenty minutes. Their eyes were riveted on the screen. Screen time had replaced interactive family time.

When the shows concluded, they reemerged—a bit out of control, voices raised and gestures aggressive. The fruit in the bowls on the table became projectiles. They were now warriors fighting ooze monsters and saving the world, replicating what they had experienced on-screen.

My wife had an idea. She moved the table in front of the couch to the wall and pointed the lamps toward the center of the room. "Let's put on our own show," she suggested, and asked the kids to put on their Halloween superhero costumes. Within minutes our granddaughter returned dressed head to toe in her emboldened Supergirl outfit. Our grandson came back clothed as Spider-Man, face mask and all. Then, a show of another making unfolded. The virtual superheroes whom they had been watching on-screen were now enacted in embodied child's play.

Imaginations ignited, they danced, tumbled, and interacted with each other and with us. One storyline evolved into the next for almost an hour. Each area of that room was newly imagined, becoming a distant land, a seascape. Together, as a family, we participated in a living theater that included each of us as well as the screen lives of the action figures.

We were back in touch. The virtual guests of Supergirl and Spider-Man were now part of our family life. The new stories were rooted in our personal imaginations and our family's enactment. And my wife and I found, to our surprise and delight, that incorporating the screen lives of action figures into our family gathering offered us fresh possibilities of being together. I turned to my wife and said, "Thank you."

Engaging in touch, laughter, and play allowed us to celebrate the spontaneous outflowing of imagination and creativity. The living room became a place of human interaction, of real depth of feeling. This kind of interaction is critical to keeping alive your own and your family's authentic humanity.

Technology and Teenagers

By the teenage years, the screen can become omnipresent, and human embodied interaction becomes marginalized. In our society, new issues are emerging due to the attention teenagers give to screens versus interacting with people IRL. The current generation of digital natives are often clumsy at relating to others offline, creating anxiety and a

sense of inadequacy. I have listened to parents, teachers, and counselors across the world share painful experiences of young people not
knowing what to do in social situations. Colleges are reporting the
absence of social involvement among students. Dating has dropped,
intimate interaction (including sexual) as well as marriage and serious
partner relationships have decreased. Birth rates in many countries are
at all-time lows, and social isolation is at historic highs.[4] Of course, the
cause of these trends can be tracked to multiple variables, but in many
instances, limitations in social literacy track back to the replacement
of direct human contact with one-step-removed indirect screen usage.[5]

Once, I attended a board of education–sponsored community
forum for parents to address the phenomenon of cyberaddiction
among teenagers. It was held on a Friday night in a large venue. Every
seat was taken. I had the privilege of listening as parents from multicultural backgrounds and diverse income levels shared their stories in
small groups with one another.

A couple named Joe and Mary stood up to address the group. "We
just do not know what to do," said Joe. "Our fourteen-year-old daughter, Sally, never leaves her room. And when she does, she is constantly
on her phone, even at the dinner table." Mary chimed in to share about
their sixteen-year-old son. "Paul seems so despondent most of the time,"
she said. "We don't know if he has any real friends, other than whoever
he is interacting with online. The door to his room is always closed. I
hear the sounds of guns and bombs, as well as loud voices. I am not sure
what is happening. I am frightened for him, big time."

More parents joined in with experiences about their once joyful,
now noncommunicative children. Of course, the phenomenon is in
part a natural effect of the teenage years, when the age-old human need
to separate from parental structures kicks in. Yet we all know there is
more to the story; these examples clearly show the impact technology
has on our very humanity.

The way forward, once again, is not to eliminate the machine, but
rather to establish a cocreative relationship. I saw this cocreation when

I had the dream of the Woman with Translucent Screens. The woman and the machine were merged. The woman assisted by technology had the capacity to be deeply human and had a new way of being in community.

The Woman with Translucent Screens

Several years back, while I was walking through the fjords of New Zealand, my imagination awakened with a set of images that came to me quite suddenly: an image of a new habitat, with a different kind of community. That night, this dream came forward.

I find myself in a community of people I do not know, in a diverse neighborhood composed of people of different backgrounds and socioeconomic levels. Then, something surprising and intriguing happens: a Woman with Translucent Screens affixed to her body welcomes me. She is radiant. I am in awe of her. I notice that each person has a set of translucent display screens embedded in their bodies. Each screen shows aspects of their state of being. One displays emotions; another, their spiritual dimension; another, their relational predisposition; while still another, their desires; and another, their inner conflicts. What is so curious is that these screens have transparence and leave little to make assumptions about, nor are there unrevealed secrets to feed hurtful or misplaced projections. The harmony within the community is very evident. The screens are machines, sophisticated cybertechnology, that act as tools to make visible the inner complexity of everyone in the community. Personal interaction thus takes place at both the interpersonal verbal and the transpersonal nonverbal level.

In the dream, the woman continues to companion me in a deeply empathetic way. I have a sense of the future showing itself through her presence. In her neighborhood, there is no concern for a lack of individual imagination, nor a loss of autonomy or individuality. To the contrary, the deep humanity of each neighbor is on full display. The genius alive in each person shines through.

Upon waking, I thought that these images were offering information about many aspects of my own personality and circumstances in life. However, I realized that what I experienced was beyond the personal: it was a new vision in which communication was both human to human and through unique computer screens. Bringing a witnessing presence to the multiplicity of translucent screens, I no longer saw through a singular lens, but rather through the multidimensionality of the imagining psyche.

When you are seeing through the multiplicity of lenses, you are arguably in the place of poetic expression. Now, if the Imagination Matrix System is engaged, it aids in the highest forms of creative human endeavors—writing, music, art, invention, movement. This is the field where your Soul Companions exist. Here you experience their spontaneity and their poetry. Also, you cocreatively reconnect with and deepen into your essential humanity. This is the antidote to tech burnout.

This happened with Julie, a young graphic designer I met when consulting at a social media firm in San Francisco. Like most of her colleagues, she worked at her computer more than ten hours a day, often six days a week. In the beginning, Julie felt the job connected to her artistic expression and a sense of fulfilling her life purpose. However, by the time I met her a few years later, things had changed decidedly for the worse. She shared with me that she was burned out, feeling numb and without direction. "I am doing my job hour after hour. I am beginning to feel like a robot," she said. "I feel that I am being taken over by the very machine that I spend so much time working on." As much as that tool enabled expression in remarkable ways, Julie's experience was separating her from her essential humanity. She felt dull and joyless, as did many of her colleagues. She said to me, "I live more in cyberspace than I do in my human space."

When sitting with Julie, I felt her despair and desperation. Then she mentioned, "You know, it was not always like this. I used to sketch and paint just for the fun of it. That is how I got into this field." I spent the next half hour exploring these experiences with Julie, inviting her to say more about what opened in her when she remembered "the fun of it." She described a time when her creativity emerged without needing to conform to an agenda, deadline, or external expectation.

I recommended that Julie take the next two weeks to allow herself to witness. She began to cry. "Wow, I don't know what just happened," she said. "I'm feeling rushes of emotion." Julie was coming home to what she remembered as her natural talent.

I recommended Julie play anthropologist for the next two weeks and witness the multiplicity of perspectives when they occurred. Julie took the time to notice her waking and night dreams, events and conversations occurring in her primary relationship, and circumstances from her workplace. She was to add these to her journal as field notes. When I met Julie the next time, I could see a bit of sparkle returning to her eyes. I suggested that she take a long weekend to make a collage with materials inspired from guidance given by the Four Quadrants of the Imagination Matrix System. From Earth, it could be a leaf, flower, or the like. From Mind, it could be a poem, a phrase, or an idea. From Machine could come computer-generated graphics or something similar. And from the Universe, it could be the experience of the sunrise, the sunset, or the night sky.

After the weekend, Julie recounted that she had loved the "high play" exercise. She also decided she could take this exercise into her workplace. She organized a group gathering of colleagues on Tuesday and Thursday mornings, with full support of the company's leadership team. They set up a space where each person would paint, draw, sketch, and collaborate with others, person to person, without a machine interface. Six months later, she reported that the quality of her life had improved considerably, and, moreover, the morale and quality of contact between colleagues had also shifted in a more human direction.

Feeling Overtaken by Tech: The Quick Shift Protocol

Open your Curious Mind. Identify a scene from nature, a particular experience, or a dream that captivates your curiosity.

Write it down. Take a few moments and describe in writing what has greeted you. Now write the passage out a second time without the punctuation, capital letters, and paragraph breaks. Let the description take on a life of its own.

Notice what begins to stand out. Write this section one last time, this time through a multiplicity of perspectives. In a few short phrases, allow adjectives, symbols, analogies, and/or metaphors to come forward and lead the way. Don't overthink it—allow the poetic expression to emerge.

Reflect. Place your creation in front of you. Experience its resonance. Slow down, breathe, and read it out loud. Listen for what emerges on the lines and between the lines.

Embrace. Experience your human spontaneity and joy opening from within. Relax and allow your smile to widen.

The State of Flow

As we move forward today into the next age of technology, we have a unique ability that will help us sustain our humanity, even as we embrace new technologies. This is what is called *the state of flow*. It is the last bastion of what makes us human. Being in flow is equivalent to raising your theta waves and journeying in the realms of deep imagination. Researchers have described the characteristics of flow as including engagement, immediacy, joy, and optimized well-being and productivity.[6]

Flow originates in the Confluence of the Imagination Matrix. It is the energetic force that awakens when the Four Quadrants are in harmonic balance. From Earth we get the generative spontaneity of the life force. From Mind we experience the wellsprings of limitless creativity, the fluidity of the Soul Companions. From Machine we touch into the facilitation between technology and its users. From the Universe we receive the awe present in the cosmic flow. When you attain Confluence among these aspects, you experience the state of flow.

Gliding Pelican

I experienced being in a state of flow recently when walking along the beach near my home. Even though the sea was calm, the waves low, and the beach tranquil, my mind was busy. I walked with urgency as my thoughts sped along to organize the list of loose ends, obligations, and chores that I needed to complete before getting to the weekend. It was as if by picking up my pace, I thought I could get these tasks done more quickly. I was barely present to the slower, more harmonic rhythms of the oceanscape in front of me.

In the midst of my rational mind's frantic scramble, a huge pelican caught my eye. Its long wings outstretched, it glided through the sky above me. My attention shifted, and my curiosity awakened. My eyes followed the pelican as the sea breezes supported its flight. Then, suddenly, it retracted its wings and narrowed its body. With its eyes riveted on something below, it dove straight down into the ocean.

Over the years, I have witnessed pelicans do this many times. However, on this day, in the diffuse sunlight of the late afternoon, something new opened inside of me. My Curious Mind became engaged with the wonder of this beautiful creature and the natural world around us. I felt that I, too, had the ability to glide in harmony with the winds. My actions were no longer generated by rational thought, but by my connection to the universal source. I was in the state of flow.

By attuning to the Imaginal harmony, I was able to see the wider expanse of the sky above and the landscape below in detail. Like the pelican, I could perceive the particulars: the fish, the shells, the ocean waves rolling toward shore. My body became relaxed. I felt attuned to an energetic field fused together by the elements of Earth, Mind, Machine, and Universe.

As I allowed the experience of flow to move through me, a deeply felt phenomenon occurred. The moveable parts of my schedule started to find their own harmonious orchestration. The state of flow and the Imagination Matrix brought me to a new possible that I could not have perceived through my rational mind alone.

The pelican glided down to the waters in front of me once more. For those precious moments, everything around me was part of a life experience animated by imagination. At the beach, I was reminded that when we sustain our connection to the playful genius of the Curious Mind, our rational defenses soften. In these moments, we are gifting both ourselves and others with nothing less than love. I smiled at the bird, acknowledging the gifts it brought to me that afternoon, and then went about my day.

Accessing Flow: The Quick Shift Protocol

This is a four-step praxis for shifting away from the busy mind into a state of flow. Find a quiet place to do this practice.

Follow Curiosity. Give yourself an ample amount of time to record your thoughts in a journal. Write down as many of the details of the situation and/or mindset that you are in right now as you can. Be honest and observe what comes up, even if what arises has a deep intensity. At times the experience can be joyful; at other times, painful. Stay with whatever comes forward.

Hold the image. Let the image come to life and gain its numinosity.

Let it dance. Attune your body to the presence of the resonating image. Let yourself move with its rhythms and participate in the energetic dance.

Experience flow. Continue in the rhythm unfolding between you and the image. When you feel the urge to stop, take a breath and allow the process between the two of you to continue for a little while longer. You are opening a reciprocity, a fluidity. This is the state of flow.

Imaginal Exchange

When you are aligned with the Imagination Matrix, you experience a fluidity with your humanity, not a fear of being taken over by the overdetermination of any one of the Four Quadrants—particularly that of the Machine. In this mode of consciousness, you befriend your Soul Companions with their magic and potency. As the figures of your soul life come into visibility and become embodied, your sense of identity broadens as well. You begin living in the company of others. Not "I"; rather, "we."

You are no longer alone, living through technology. In Confluence, which energizes the state of flow, the multiple aspects of the whole are balanced. You become the one and the many. A cultivated inner life offers a renewed sense of joy. The door has been opened; the way through is to Follow Curiosity. You feel your deep belonging, not fear. With a sense of groundedness, psyche alive, tools at hand, and a feeling of limitless connection, you nurture and sustain your inheritance— your humanity.

The producers of technology have a social responsibility to do what they can to create platforms that emphasize well-being and accessibility. You, as the user of this technology, have a choice in how you show up. When you choose to be genuine, deep, and soulful on social media, the people in your networks take notice.

This Imaginal exchange between you and technology sustains and enhances both. Spending time inside the state of flow and the Imagination Matrix, you begin to see through the material world into the metaphorical and Imaginal realms that connect all being. Following the hints you find there, you access deeper and wider dimensions of your creativity and your humanity. You begin to attune to the Story-Web underpinning the Imagination Matrix. It is through this very human process that you can move bravely into the next iteration of life on earth.

Chapter 11

The Story-Web

You have arrived. And you are at the beginning. Your Curious Mind is activated; your perception, open and receptive. Now revealed behind the veil of the Imagination Matrix is what I call the *Story-Web*, which underpins all. This vast interactive network of metapatterns holds the interconnection of ideas, myths, and dreams across space and time. The Story-Web resonates with the sound of the universe that is in perpetual motion. From this cacophony emerges the Awakening Story, which speaks to the present but most importantly conveys the pull of the future. The Awakening Story is simultaneously your personal story and the stories you know and love, sometimes inspiring and sometimes difficult, that were passed down from the elders or hints from the future just now arriving. In your engagement with the Awakening Story, you realize that what you once attributed to hunch or simple deduction is part of a much greater truth. What gets Illuminated in these interactions opens innovation and the emergent possible.

The source language of the Imagination Matrix is story. But unlike the narratives that are by and large imposed on you from other people's or institutional expectations and judgments, the stories that come forward from the Imagination Matrix are more generative, heart-opening, and perspective-expanding. You can spot the difference in these ways.

Stories that come at you today from external sources in our culture, such as social media, might operate from a hidden motivation to get you to purchase a product, sway you to a belief, or gain visibility for a particular influencer. They are narratives that push you toward a preprogrammed life plan, often one in which you have already failed in some way—are you rich enough, pretty enough, thin enough, perfect enough? These kinds of stories, based on lack and not on the abundance found in the Imagination Matrix, abound online and elsewhere in our culture. They can often take hold in your mind in destructive ways, causing dysfunctional patterns in relationships and self-care.

Stories originating in the Imagination Matrix, on the other hand, are often metaphoric, poetic, and sometimes dramatic. Stories generated in the upwellings of your Imaginal journeys widen your perspectives, rather than narrow them. They tell of your true purpose, your heart's desire. They arrive in many forms—instructive fables, teaching parables, healing fictions, and more. They often have multitextual symbolic layers. Culturally, these stories of the depths are the stuff of myth and mythmaking. As Joseph Campbell offers, "Myth is the secret opening through which the inexhaustible energies of the cosmos pour into human manifestation."[1] Neil deGrasse Tyson casts it in this way: "We are stardust, brought to life, then empowered by the universe to figure itself out—and we have only just begun."[2] Your story is being woven right now. When you feel caught in the circumstances of life or, conversely, when you are inspired, you have the opportunity to become aware of the Story-Web.

The Story-Web

In the tradition of depth psychology, the *mundis imaginalis* and the *intersubjective imaginal field* are concepts used to describe dimensions of existence—the worlds behind the world. When you access the Imagination Matrix, you can perceive the patterns of the universal Story-Web in all their beauty. You begin to see the Illuminated world in which everything is dreaming and imagining. You experience all phenomena, creatures, landscapes, and things (not just people) as having subjective interiority. When you perceive metaphorically and poetically, it's not what you see but, rather, how you see what you see. All beings, animate and inanimate, have stories to tell.

I met Andrea when she came to one of my workshops on imagination. She had always wondered about the role imagination played in her business acumen. Andrea is a very successful real estate agent in Santa Barbara who has sold homes in some of the toniest neighborhoods in town. Andrea has found buyers for more homes year after year than most anybody else.

People, particularly those in her industry, frequently ask her, "How do you do it?" They wonder about her method, her secret. During our workshop, Andrea shared that even as a little girl she had the ability to hear stories in landscapes and places. She would walk around her neighborhood at a slow pace, pausing in front of houses and yards. "Their stories would come to me," she said. "Some were sad, others seemed happy, while a few were in a state of distress at the separation from the people who once dwelled within."

Now as an adult in the business of selling homes, Andrea still listened deeply to the stories coming through both the properties and the persons. She knew that each home had a different story to tell, one that would often reveal a personality. Andrea felt in her core that she was not a real estate agent but a matchmaker. Andrea would feel into the intersections between the home's needs and desires and those of potential buyers to find the right match instead of merely selling houses to the highest bidder. She connected the story of the house to the story of the potential owner and to new stories that they could create together.

Andrea was intuitively engaging the Imagination Matrix and the Awakening Stories from the Story-Web. In taking the time to slow down and open her Curious Mind to the unseen interconnections, she made a very real difference. Upon leaving the workshop, Andrea said that she felt understood.

Andrea continues to do what she always has done. Leading with her Curious Mind, Andrea contributes to the new Awakening Stories of buyer, seller, and home. In this way, Andrea engages the Imagination Matrix and the Story-Web in her work. It is natural to her, like breathing. Her sales success continues to climb at a record pace.

Foundational Template: Evoking the Story-Web

Begin. Start by opening your Curious Mind. Go into your Dig. Take the time to listen to whatever story is moving through you here and now. Often it is useful to have a supporting presence, like a pet, friend, partner, or one of your Soul Companions, alongside you.

Allow. The story you hear has a life of its own. You might have heard this story before. Perhaps it is a recurring story, like a life script voicing over and over a judgmental or critical opinion. Perhaps you hear a story of encouragement, support, and care. Allow whatever story is there to come forward.

Make the space. Write the story down. Let the flow of the story move with its own rhythm and cadence. In this exercise, it is good to first use paper and pen or pencil. The keyboard or recording device can follow.

Underline and describe. Highlight or underline the elements that comprise the story: the individual figures, landscapes, and creatures. Give description to the tone and inflection of the various voices you notice. Observe the actions taking place.

Place the different elements. Now, on a larger single page, list all the elements you've noted and pulled out from the previous step. Do not create any order per se; rather, let them come forward and place themselves wherever they land. You will notice that many of the elements naturally find a place to be situated.

Create a web. Next, notice the connections between one element in your story and the others. Extend these lines of connectivity. No need to push the river or create a preconceived design. Let the pattern that connects reveal itself on its own behalf—not in a content-oriented way, but rather in a process-based manner. Let the Story-Web emerge.

Personify. Notice the Story-Web coming to life on its own behalf. What colors and shapes does it take? Imagine the wind blowing through the web. What story do you hear coming through now? Close your eyes and see the Awakening Story.

Tuning in to the Story-Web

Once attuned to the Story-Web, you notice that the tellers of the essential stories are those you have encountered in your journeying through the realms of deep imagination. As you have experienced, these Soul Companions come with multiple emotional perspectives, additional modes of perception, and varied styles of sensate and spiritual responsiveness. These figures and settings exist behind the familiar narratives of everyday routine. In their presence, your life opens to the larger story, to the Story-Web with its many new storylines. No longer are you the single main character playing the role and speaking the lines of a narrow life script. In the Story-Web you are more than a singular figure; you are, in fact, the full novel.

Opening the Doors

From the beginning of time, stories embedded within the prime material of the realms of deep imagination have emerged through the Story-Web. These emergent stories have an autonomy of their own. They contain elements originating from each quadrant—Earth, Mind, Machine, Universe—which combine to generate interrelated stories. These teaching stories are possible for you to both access and listen into for guidance. They offer support, insight, and deeper connection to yourself and others.

Each of the Four Quadrants opens a portal into the Story-Web. In addition, each quadrant serves as a home ground, offering valuable elements to the stories located in the Story-Web. Consider both the elements inherent to each quadrant as well as the contributions each quadrant makes to the stories inherent to the whole Story-Web. Remember, there are countless formulations, unlimited elements.

Discover Your Awakening Story

The Imagination Matrix System provides valuable perspectives. Open your Curious Mind and allow the many possibilities to come into your awareness. Invite your Awakening Story to emerge. Begin as always with your Quadrant Work.

Quadrant Work: Asking Orienting Questions

Earth. Is there a particular setting that is foundational to your dreams or stories? How do the regenerative qualities of nature give birth to your own aspirations? (These questions are based on the idea that in an animated world, the landscapes, animals, and ecosystems each have a story to tell.)

Mind. How is your story connected to archetypal stories of the collective psyche? How are the characters personifications of mythology, fairy tales, legends, and folklore? (These questions originate in the idea that the language of imagination is metaphoric and expresses itself through story.)

Machine. How does your daily interaction with machines influence the stories that you experience? What impact do the new technologies have on the stories that you tell yourself and others? (These questions originate in the idea that the Machine Quadrant is an essential component of the Imagination Matrix.)

Universe. What mysteries do the images of story bring to your imagination? How does your Illuminated Consciousness get both announced and cultivated through story? (These questions originate in the concept that transcendent principles orchestrate the Imagination Matrix.)

Quadrant Work: Receiving Insights

Earth. The Earth Quadrant brings the ever-renewing qualities of Gaia into the stories. Characters, landscapes, and elements become personified through animals, like coyote and wolf; through fertile landscapes, like the jungle and the ocean waters; and through elements, like quicksilver and gold. The Earth Quadrant brings grounding to stories, the location where action takes place, the path on which you adventure.

Mind. Whereas the Earth provides the ground of origination, the Mind Quadrant offers Imaginal motifs found in the archetypal patterning of the collective psyche. From this quadrant we source Imaginal characters who are both participants in and originators of the stories. The Imaginal figures bring awareness to other characters, settings, emotions, and activities that have an archetypal meaning, a collective mythic quality.

Machine. The functionality and fluidity of the Machine Quadrant brings locomotion and hybrid intelligence to stories. Characters and motifs that are generated from the Machine Quadrant depict the fusion between mechanical and human capabilities.

Universe. This quadrant announces the call of an Illuminated Consciousness. This is sourced in the universal connection of the cosmos, of all dimensions of time and space. In conjunction with Earth, Mind, and Machine, the Universe Quadrant reflects the multiplicity of perspectives to help you see the interactivity present in the bigger picture, the dance of the spheres.

Attaining Confluence: Integrating the New Possible

You now enhance and intertwine your personal stories with the arche-typal patterns of the collective story. You weave these together with insights from the Four Quadrants into new narratives that frame your Awakening Story. Nighttime and waking dreams and visions reveal these storylines. Your Awakening Story is one of the infinite number of Awakening Stories of the Story-Web.

Goanna Dreaming

I had the experience of being part of a larger story, both as an observer and as a participant, when journeying with my family in the Outback of Australia. In the most expansive of ways, yet grounded in the actu-ality of family life when we were much younger, I connected with the Story-Web and, in turn, with my destiny.

During my first sabbatical, a special time out of time when I was on leave from my administrative and teaching responsibilities, I traveled to Australia with my family. Going Down Under became both a lived and an Imaginal experience. Academically, I was doing research on the Dreamtime and seeking guidance from Aboriginal elders. How naïve; how Western. What ended up happening was indeed an immersion into the Innate Genius of the Aboriginal Dreamtime but was by no means the formal academic research I had imagined. Rather, in the end, the Story-Web alive in the landscape reached out and touched my family's lives forever.

Shortly after arrival in Darwin, we drove outside the city for a day hike. Within minutes we found ourselves in the backcountry of the Northern Territories, the land of the Aboriginal Dreamtime. Unaware of what awaited us, we ventured ever forward: my seven-year-old son, my four-year-old daughter, and my wife, who was pregnant at the time. At midday, we set up our picnic lunch on a stunning rock ledge above a small waterfall. While we ate peanut-butter-and-honey rice cakes, we heard a rustling sound at the water's edge. Always wary of crocodiles, we got up to look and, indeed, saw a scaly reptile at least four feet long. Its tongue darted in and out as it determinedly made its way toward us. Suddenly we realized that this wasn't a crocodile at all. It was, in fact, a giant carnivorous goanna lizard. Unbeknown to us at the time, the Story-Web and the Imagination Matrix were reaching out and making their presence known.

At first, I was delighted to see a wild goanna. Clearly, this meant we were now truly in the untamed landscape of Australia. As I looked more closely at it, I saw that it noticed me. And instead of shying away, it kept coming nearer. I could feel my wife getting edgy. My daughter began screaming. I, of course, acting in perfect script, took charge and tried to chase the goanna away. But it kept coming right at us. I picked up a stick and pounded it on the ground, but the undaunted goanna stayed on course.

We grabbed our things and scurried more than two hundred yards up the riverbank, over the falls, to a new area. Free from the goanna, we set up our picnic. Suddenly my daughter screamed again and yelled, rather hysterically, "Goanna is back!" Sure enough, the determined animal had followed us up the river, over the rocks, through the water, beyond the falls, and to within a few feet of where we were sitting. Now, it became personal.

I found a bigger stick and pounded it on the ground, trying my best to manifest the image of a huge, threatening gorilla. I yelled and made loud growling sounds. As it got right up to my feet, I waved my arms and growled even more fiercely at it. Right then, the goanna jumped up and bit me on the wrist! Shocked, I shook it off and jumped away. But the goanna again lurched toward me. I shouted to my wife, "Get the kids away from here!" Everyone began running for the car, hundreds of yards away.

As we hightailed it out of there, my daughter once again screamed, "Goanna is back!" The damned lizard was chasing us! Pregnant wife and all, we somehow managed to outrun it to the car, and we drove away secure in the feeling that we had left the goanna behind for good. But not fully . . .

This experience was so surreal, so unusual, that I began to wonder what was going on behind the scenes, so to speak. Who was this goanna that was chasing my family? Was there a deeper meaning? After all, we were in the place of the Dreamtime mysteries, where Indigenous peoples have had access to the power of the Imagination Matrix and the Story-Web for centuries.

Later on in the trip, I was so fortunate to spend time with Bill Neidjie, an elder of the Aboriginal Dreamtime and perhaps one of the last surviving native speaker of the Gaagudju language. I brought this question to him. He responded at length in Gaagudju; fortunately, there were two university linguists who could interpret. They said to me, "We have never heard Bill share as much with somebody outside the clan, and it was a privilege to listen." Then, they translated what he said: "Ancestral spirits have made a visitation. Goanna has much to tell you. You have much to learn. There are special dreaming places where the power of imagination exists in the landscape, one of which was named Goanna Dreaming. Go there, remember to listen, and experience what greets you."

I reflected on what this Aboriginal elder was instructing me to do. I remembered that the power of imagination expresses itself in many forms: through dream, reverie, enactment, and now the landscape itself. Each of us encounters the Imagination Matrix differently and in multiple ways. I now see that I was experiencing its vast underlying Story-Web through the goanna.

After leaving Bill and his extended clan, my son and I took to the dirt roads and traveled further north to the Aboriginal lands where Goanna Dreaming was located. As we got closer, we could see out toward the horizon a large rock outcrop. It was unmistakable: there in the blue hue of a wide-open Australian sky sat a giant goanna lizard. The formation of red, orange, and brown rock looked as much like a goanna as the animal that had chased my family. We were in the living presence of Goanna.

At the dreaming place itself, I felt greeted by something or someone familiar yet in other ways entirely new. The place seemed sculpted over millennia by the genius of imagination. It happens that way on occasion, where the ground we stand on seems to resonate with an innate intelligence of its own, where the Story-Web behind the familiar reveals itself. There is nothing really to do other than to be in presence. Without words, I simply stood silently for a time, then walked about the rock formation mindfully. I never had a flash of insight, nor did I receive words of wisdom; rather, I felt a pulsing through my body. I did not understand what was happening but did comprehend a dimension of another kind.

I left Australia several days after this experience, knowing that something powerful had happened to me there. But what? I still didn't really understand what or how to make any sense of it all. What occurred was beyond the pale of any psychological interpretation I had ever learned. The Story-Web had made its presence known. And it wasn't over yet. A story beyond my making was unfolding, and I was but one of the participants, certainly not the creator.

Upon returning to Santa Barbara, our third child, who experienced the journey of Australia from the inside, was born. As an infant, he did something quite peculiar: when he slept with us at night, he would, with some assertion, waddle about until he'd wind up on top of my head. It was as if a pillow was over my face, his head on one side and legs on the other. At first, I pushed him off gently, but as night after night his waddling went on, my pushing got more assertive. As did his insistence on his perch. As weeks turned into months, I started using my legs to literally force him back into the center of the bed. And still, he would always crawl back on top of me.

Then one morning, my wife looked at me and exclaimed, "Steve, goanna is back!" Suddenly, I understood what was going on with my son. I stopped thinking he might be troubled in some way. Instead, I realized that, through the Story-Web, the teaching story offered in Australia was being enacted over and again. Our son was behaving like the creature that crawled over the rocks in Australia—the one that is known for its ability to climb up trees to grab food. Seemingly asking for attention, the deeper story was expressing its desire to be listened to, to be known.

For our son, the goanna might be a totem animal. After all, he did experience all that transpired in Australia, though from a unique perspective; his Imaginal Intelligence was shaped in part by our time Down Under. To this day, as I watch my son climb tall trees, hike steep mountains, and use his determination in business and relationships, I remember the spirit of the goanna and witness in my son the power of imagination that followed us home all those years ago.

For me, as well, the sparks embedded in the figures of the Story-Web continued to inform my behavior and ignite an Illuminated Consciousness many times over. Often, when least expected. I share one of these instances from my own life to underscore how, when we are attuned to the energy of the Story-Web, even when the particulars are not visible, extraordinary experiences occur. The ever-present vitality of the Story-Web manifests in ways that shape your destiny and Illuminate your purpose.

When experiences like this happen for you, I invite you to consider bringing heightened awareness to the unfolding without needing to know the cause, certainly not the meaning. Simply take in what is happening fully and be with your patience and Follow Curiosity.

Once you experience the telling of a story, the Story-Web does not stop generating original stories that can have a meaningful impact on your life. It is not static. To keep the harmonic of the Story-Web vibrant, return time and again to its ever-unfolding rhythms. Make time in your life to bring attention and attune to the imaginative stories alive behind the routine. Remember, in the ordinary exists the extraordinary. Bill Neidjie encouraged the next generations to stay close to the Story-Web:

The story is important.
It won't change,
It is like this earth,
It won't move.[3]

Foundational Template: Opening to the Story-Web

I have found over the years that one doesn't have to travel far to open oneself to the Story-Web. Stories are told many times over. Each time you listen, you experience new fascination. Through the story, you're journeying in the Imagination Matrix. With your Curious Mind open, take the time to listen with interest. It can be done anywhere. But here are some steps that will help you access the Story-Web with more ease.

Be fluid. Tune in to your Curious Mind. Allow yourself to be comfortable with the not-knowing. To be fluid opens the imagination to a quality of presence that does not exist when you hasten to reach the answer or outcome.

Be patient. Train yourself to relax and breathe, which counters the fear of being out of control. This sounds easy, perhaps, but of course it is not. We are habituated to use our rational mind and get to the bottom of things. We've forgotten how to pause and absorb what is truly present. But if we stop, if we pause, something incredible happens. We begin to see and experience the beauty and animating vitality around us, and we witness the creatures, landscapes, and things of the world in their imaginative display. The beauty, the smiles, on the faces of all beings offer their stories.

Go on a walkabout. *Walkabout* is a term used in the Outback of Australia for experiencing the dreaming and imagination of the landscape itself. It is also referred to as "temporary mobility."[4] You can do something similar to walkabout in the familiar-seeming landscape of your own location. Let yourself meet what you encounter without an agenda. Wherever you are—in the country, the city, your neighborhood—leave the list of to-dos at home, and give your cell phone a time-out. With an open mind and deepening breath, become part of the imagination of whatever Illuminates around you.

Yield to the Story-Web. Let yourself be in the story, rather than trying to dominate it. Like a naturalist, in your walkabout, simply observe and receive what is out there fully. A daily practice of just twenty minutes of this kind of walkabout shifts your perception. The landscapes, creatures, and all beings of the world offer their Imaginal presence and their Awakening Stories back to your own. In turn, the power of imagination opens your wonder, deepens your quality of life, and helps you find your right place in the world.

Envision. Keep an ongoing journal of the many characters, places, and experiences that come forward through the Story-Web in nighttime and daytime dreams, visions, and creative expression. Look for a common element or consistent theme. Write down or doodle these in no particular order. In both medium and style, be as faithful as possible to the nature of their presentation.

Connect to your destiny. Just as you might follow the journey of a lead player in a film, novel, television series, or play, notice what is referred to as the character arc that runs through your story as revealed through the Story-Web. How does this through line, which is made up of elements from the whole, resonate with aspects of your personal story? Where are the intersections, the complementarities? Can you identify any synchronicities between the story that arose through the Story-Web and events or circumstances in your awake life? Take time to pause when you experience the intersections. Through these moments of congruence you glimpse your life purpose, your destiny.

The Way of the Spider

I worked with Ed, a man in his fifties, during a Dream Tending and Imagination retreat. In one of our sessions, Ed shared an image that came to him. In a dream, he saw a sheet of white paper with a small black dot on one side. On the other side something was emerging through the paper. As he looked more closely, Ed got a quick glimpse of something crawling through the page. It seemed to be a spider, but it was not yet fully formed. No matter how he turned the page, he was only able to see a small round object that was trying to come into existence. When Ed woke up, he felt that there was a message in this dream. He wanted to understand more but didn't know what to do.

I suggested that he close his eyes. I then walked him through the tools to access the Imagination Matrix System. I asked him to think about the dream image again and allow himself to explore it once again. Now, with his Curious Mind engaged, he noticed that on the page there were the faint outlines of a web. Then, ever so slowly, a very small spider emerged and made its way across the web. It beckoned him to follow as it gathered its stories from all parts of the web near and far.

He realized that the message from his dream was to mimic the way of the spider in his waking life, feeling the pulse of stories as they emerged slowly and spontaneously from the Imagination Matrix that he was inside of and that surrounds us all. Once he was able to perceive how in a spider's web the many threads intersect in multiple ways, Ed found that he could design a more comprehensive solution to any issue.

It is not surprising that the messenger in the dream was a spider. Throughout human experience, in mythology and folklore, spiders have represented multiple inferences. The spider has symbolized patience and persistence because of its ability to create its webs. On the other hand, when a spider crosses your path, because of its sometimes poisonous venom, it could suggest oncoming malice or mischief. In West African Ashanti mythology as well as Native American Lakota legend, Spider is viewed as a trickster and the spinner of tales.[5]

I met with Ed again ten days later. He was continuing to practice "the way of the spider," walking through his often busy life at a slower, more spontaneous pace and imagining that he was traversing situations as if on a web. Keeping his curiosity activated, he noticed how circumstances intersected in patterns that connected more than he had first perceived. He shared, "It was as if I was participating in life at a deeper level. Like the spider in my dream, I was transversing through a web of consciousness below the surface of the obvious. As I slowed down, I saw things differently and heard new stories being told at the many intersections of the Story-Web."

Soul Companion the Storyteller

The human imagination has always been captured by stories. A new Soul Companion now accompanies you on this journey. This is the Storyteller who helps you stand in your authenticity and uncover the story of your destiny. The Storyteller, as a conveyer of wisdom, the memories of our ancestors, and the dreams and hopes of each generation, resonates with all of us in a primal way. A Soul Companion, the Storyteller entertains, frightens, enthralls, and connects us to the myths, legends, and mysteries relating to the present, past, and future of collective experience. As one Illuminated Storyteller, William Shakespeare, offered, "We know what we are, but know not what we may be."[6]

Claiming its central role, the Storyteller emerges through the veil. The Imagination Matrix has constituted this most essential Soul Companion, the teller of the narratives moving through you. It may surprise you that the Storyteller is not a singular figure. The Storyteller is the one and the many. They are the multiplicity of voices and stories that emerge through the Story-Web.

By experiencing the paradox of the one and the many, you find needed guidance to crystalize your own narrative. In many contemporary cultures we are habituated to look for and listen to the primary figure, the leader, the heroic presence who speaks with authority. In the Story-Web underlying the Imagination Matrix, the singular hero's journey is not the way. Rather, it is to be found in the many voices and stories of humans, landscapes, and animals. Like other Soul Companions, the Storyteller exists in both personal and archetypal dimensions. When Illuminated, the Storyteller offers cultural wisdom drawn from the stories of the collective elements of Earth, Mind, Machine and Universe. Tribal elders, poets, literary masters, and musical prodigies are but a few of the people through whom these stories are shared; folktales, legends, fables, and musical scores are a few of the forms.

As the central Soul Companion, the Storyteller is the presence who awakens imagination and the stories that you tell yourself. Sometimes experienced as that ongoing voice inside, that North Star which directs you, the Storyteller holds you enthralled with its transformational powers. As such, the Storyteller in all of its aspects is a Soul Companion by its very nature and, when Illuminated, guides you to your Awakening Story.

The Storyteller: Master Weaver
(Orchestrator, Narrator, Oracle)

When you are in relationship with the Storyteller, your life is animated. Stories are ever present, told in the ways of adventure or fantasy, romance or tragedy. Of course, there are stories generated by other figures, such as Monster or Vampire. But here at the center of the Story-Web, the Storyteller becomes the primary figure. In this way, the Storyteller is the dream weaver, orchestrator, narrator, and oracle informing your purpose and the fate of the planet.

When Illuminated, the Storyteller gives voice and embodiment to what exists at the intersections in the Imagination Matrix. The Storyteller accesses the elements of the Four Quadrants, then weaves this knowledge into Awakening Stories to be listened to by people worldwide. The Illuminated Storyteller originates in the many figures alive in the Story-Web and, too, gives voice to the whole of the Story-Web itself.

The Illuminated Storyteller functions as a chrysalis, which holds the essence of all things and operates in the multiplicity of perception and space/time. This seems to be what happened with Albert Einstein, who found the ability to access the mystery of the Imagination Matrix.

Jean Houston, renowned author and philosopher, met Einstein when she was a young girl. The encounter touched her deeply. During a Pacifica Institute lecture, she described what he shared with her that day: "Einstein told me that when he was only four years old, he jumped into the fire of the imagination. He said that his journeys took him to the far reaches of the universe. The stories he heard in imagination informed his conceptual formulations of how multiple realities intersected."[7]

Through the multiplicity of perspectives found in the Imagination Matrix, the habituated patterns of the world start to give way as something new is being born. In older traditions, the Gnostics, Kabbalists, magi, Daoists, Dakinis, and other persons esteemed as having direct knowledge of the hidden divinity attained via mystical insight also connected to the Imagination Matrix. In uncovering the Illuminated Storyteller, they shared stories that originated behind the veil and brought forward the wisdom and insights of the Four Quadrants.

When you listen to your Illuminated Storyteller weave the tales that are moving through the Imagination Matrix, you at once recognize the emergent impulse that informs your calling. You hear into the deeper possibilities.

Commitment to Yourself: Accessing the World Through the Story-Web

As the bond between you and the Illuminated Storyteller evolves, both of you experience the growing regard that fills your relationship. As the Storyteller Illuminates, so does your Illuminated Consciousness. This two-way gifting is nothing less than an act of unconditional love.

Through this love-centered relationship, the Storyteller is taking you home to yourself. In receiving the gifts of guiding stories, you also receive a sense of grace. Gaining access to the Storyteller is not hard to do. The following praxis helps you deepen your relationship. Practice it again and again. Start by setting an intention: "I will evoke the

Illuminated Storyteller in my practice of accessing the world through the Story-Web."

Notice. What story lives in a deeper place beneath what you are experiencing now? Allow yourself to open to the realms that live below the surface. When you are in this process, sometimes you can bump up against negative, painful, even frightening feelings. If this is the case, enlist the support of your other allied Soul Companions to provide you the safety and protection you need to go on with your praxis.

Be present. Do not make this complicated. Simply be in the spontaneity of what is occurring.

Feel. Name what surfaces. Words like *awe, excitement, compassion, wonder, freedom,* and *courage* are but a few of the names that might show up. Whatever comes forward is good enough. Discerning these qualities is the gift you have received and the gift you will give back.

Act. Repeat this practice regularly. Doing so deepens your relationship with your Illuminated Storyteller. It will also strengthen your commitment to building your capacity to accessing the Story-Web in your daily life.

The Return Home

In quantum physics, most everything is viewed as entangled with everything else.[8] The Illuminated Storyteller possesses the capacity to perceive the interwoven stories and light your pathway forward. Like a harpist playing particular strings, the Illuminated Storyteller gives energy, sounds, and cadence to what becomes an Awakening Story— your Awakening Story. This pulsating center is where stories are birthed, dreams are made, and soul making happens.

This is the Imagination Matrix. You have arrived. And you are at the beginning. Through the Imagination Matrix system, your Curious

Mind opens to the tapestry of stories originating from the past and those yet to come. The lovers and creators as well as the outlaws and tricksters all have creative roles to play. You feel the sanctuary that comes with being a participant in the unfolding story lines of the Story-Web. You have come home.

Your preparation has led to this moment. You join a lineage extending back through your kin (your literal and Imaginal family line) and reaching forward to those who you may be meeting for the first time. When seen through Illuminated eyes (a wider perspective), all becomes imagination. You see what has always been true. Your purpose, your destiny, your own Awakening Story is connected through the Story-Web to every being on the planet. You are now cocreating the emerging future within the community of others: Soul Companions, elders and ancestors, seekers, and visionaries. In this Imaginal community, you receive the unconditional love and belonging that is every person's birthright.

Here, now, you stand rooted in the generative powers of the Imagination Matrix. It is time to face the questions: What to do? What is being asked of you?

Epilogue

The Pull of the Future

I received an invitation some years ago to the Peace Palace at The Hague in the Netherlands to participate in the United Nations-sponsored development of the Earth Charter, an international declaration of fundamental values and principles for building a just, sustainable, and peaceful global society. I joined seventy others from thirty different countries to combine our best thinking and to develop a plan that could be circulated around the world for review and comment.

This particular meeting at The Hague was cochaired by the late Mikhail Gorbachev, former leader of the Soviet Union, then president and founder of Green Cross International, and Maurice Strong, a Canadian diplomat and environmentalist.[1] At The Hague, our intention was to come up with the first draft of the charter, which we worked on for five days and nights. It turned out that I was the last to speak and was still standing at the podium when Gorbachev announced that we had failed in our most earnest efforts to come up with a plan to go forward. A hush fell over the room. The faces reflected a mixture of shock and despair.

As I stood at the podium in front of the crowd, waiting to give my closing remarks, I felt the same sadness as the others. Then another impulse moved through me from an energy source very deep inside and outside of me. I recognized the upwelling immediately. It was the same potency I had experienced at Goanna Dreaming in Australia.

Something was about to come forward, and I knew not what. It is curious how the realms of deep imagination work. Their generative expression sometimes comes out months or years later, when we least expect it. What to do? I paused, took in a breath, and simply let the words flow from a place of another making. With conviction, I declared, "Perhaps we are going about this the wrong way. Perhaps from the beginning we have been asking the wrong question."

I went on with growing confidence. "The question is not: What can we do for the earth? Rather, the relevant question we must address is: What is the planet asking of us?" I suggested that we now needed a new methodology to listen to others, to our dreams and stories; we needed to rekindle our access to deep imagination "so each of us are able to hear what's being asked of us here at this critical time."

When I finished my remarks, one of those moments happened that I will forever remember. Gorbachev, standing at the podium, looked directly at me and said, "Sir, that is the right question, now go do it." Maurice Strong agreed. "The time is now," he said. "Take what you know and birth it into the world." Those words, "birth it into the world," hit me like a lightning bolt. What had been incubating inside of me all my days was now pushing its way through me, announcing the next phase of my life's work.

The Emerging Possible

Now, decades later, we stand once again at another crossroad, one at which we are asked to summon our power of imagination to embody our Awakening Stories. Each Awakening Story contains essential guidance for planetary well-being. This essential guidance directs each person who accesses the Imagination Matrix with intention. Leading an Imagination-Centered Life has fortified your body, mind, and spirit. You have learned to open your Curious Mind, rekindle Imaginal Play, invite fun and joy into your encounters. Utilizing the Imagination Matrix System has taught you how to lead with compassion, curiosity, and innovation. It is true in all realms, the Imaginal and the incarnate, that when tending to a community, you strengthen both yourself and those around you. This is the essence of Ensouled Stewardship.

In the Imagination Matrix, the authentic originality at the heart of places, persons, things, and spirit come to be known. Each of the Four Quadrants—Earth, Mind, Machine, and Universe—reveals the soul sparks of its essential nature. Each offers its prophecy for the next evolution of humanity.

Remember that this is *your* time.

Whether a millennial or a centenarian, you know, as we all know, the world of tomorrow asks something of us today. We are reimagining our work, our creativity, our interactions with technology, and our very humanity. In this, we are pressing the reset button of history. We stand together for the well-being of all on this planet and for generations to come.

You are ready.

Now prepared, you can answer the call with courage and conviction. You have journeyed far, wide, and deep in the Imagination Matrix. This work has revealed the gifts you are meant to share in constructing a new life. You can move ahead with the knowledge of how to utilize the Imagination Matrix System in the world. I invite you to make a commitment to your ongoing practice through this Ritual of Service.

Ritual of Service

Find a quiet place that helps you center.
   —Light a candle, actually or Imaginally.

In service of the teachings received from deep imagination, repeat to yourself three times,
   —"What does the world need from me now?"

Open your Curious Mind.
Be ready for the unexpected.
Listen to your Awakening Story.

Gratitudes

To begin, I am grateful to the Soul Companions who guided and supported me in my journeys through the Imagination Matrix.

I am forever grateful to Russ Lockhart, whose wise counsel and care over the decades supported the exploration. He taught me the ways of seeing imagination.

Other mentors who invited me into their life and work include Joseph Campbell, Marion Woodman, James Hillman, Robert Johnson, Jean Houston, Robbie Bosnak, Rick Tarnas, and Michael Mead. I have been inspired by my heartfelt contact with Chinese scholar Heyong Shen, Aboriginal Elders Bill Neidjie and Yidumduma Bill Harney, Hawaiian kahuna Lulu, and Indian scholar and environmental advocate Vandana Shiva. To all of you, with humility, I build upon your work.

In addition, I am grateful to the writers, philosophers, poets, and artists that have been touched by the foundational contributions of Carl Jung and the lineage of seekers who came before and after.

To the many co-journeyers that I encountered in the Human Potentials Movement and the Counterculture of the late '60s and '70s through today, I am grateful. Your spirit of advocacy, social justice, and environmental consciousness were and continue to be formative. To the many students that I have been privileged to mentor through the years, thank you. You opened your hearts and souls which in turn deepened my own. Your desire to learn, your curiosity to question, and your courage to grow inspires the work that moves through me and onto these pages.

I am more than grateful to the many faculty, staff, students, alumni, and board members of Pacifica Graduate Institute. From inception, your love, your challenge, and your visions spark the matrix of imagination that illuminates my life.

To Claudia Riemer Boutote of Red Raven Studio, my literary guide, mentor, advocate, champion, and conductor, your orchestration over the years illuminates this work on and off the page. Your clarity, vision, and language-craft are offered through your wealth of talent and good humor. I appreciate you deeply.

I want to thank Tami Simon, founder and publisher of Sounds True, for her vision and service to the world. I am grateful to Associate Publisher Jaime Schwalb for her integrity, her commitment to this book, and for truly walking the path of ensouled leadership. My editor Haven Iverson, for her expert editorial guidance and valuable insights. Thank you to Leslie Brown, Diana Rico, and Jade Lascelles for your excellent work, and to the entire team at Sounds True.

My heartfelt appreciation extends to John Ziegler, whose artistic talent and expertise graces the cover of this book and more. To Marna Hauk, I am grateful for your academic skill, research expertise, and capacities to navigate the confluence between the arts and sciences. Your unwavering support has been so very helpful and heartfelt. Jeffrey Tarant, thank you for your guidance that made our inquiry into Imaginal Intelligence possible. To Michael Taft, whose love of the work, guidance, and mentorship over the years opened my capacities to write and tell a story, enabling the craft of Dream Tending and my journeying into imagination to be brought into the world.

To the extended Dream Tending and Imagination community, your generosity of heart and soul over the decades has nourished and graced the Soul Companions alive in the imaginal realms that bless my life. My heartfelt gratitude to the Mentors of the Dream Tending and

Academy of Imagination, thanks for all. Through your generative work, I continue to rediscover my own . . . and we are just getting started.

Special gratitude to the to the board members of the Academy of Imagination, whose commitment is to take the Imagination Matrix System into community life, the workplace, and corporate board rooms.

To my family, past, present, and future: your innate genius, your Imaginal Intelligence, and your love opens the passions of my heart's desire. To my children, Jesse, Alia, and Eli, and daughter-in-law, Karolina, your force of character fuses what lives within these covers. To my grandchildren, Samuel and Mila, and those who will follow, this book is for you. To my great grandfather, Zalman the Shoemaker, the illuminated Storyteller is of your making. And to Dora, his daughter, my grandmother, your courage continues to spark my own.

My deepest gratitude is for my wife, Maren. My journeying the limitless realms of the Imagination Matrix is anchored in the love and grounding that is of your depths. I am forever grateful.

Glossary

Alpha wave: Brain waves indicating the active mind (thinking, ego), alertness, and possibly stressful states of attention and problem-solving modes.

Awakening Story: Simultaneously your story and the interwoven stories of the present, past, and what will be. Evolving from the Story-Web, the Awakening Story carries the pull of the future, revealing the greater truth of your destiny and the planet's becoming.

Confluence: The energetic threads of the Four Quadrants (Earth, Mind, Machine, Universe), which are ever reshaping and reconnecting, fuse at multiple points of Confluence. Each Confluence provides the energy that sparks inspiration and propels innovation. The Confluence is the ever-generating birthplace of the new possible.

Curious Mind: A mode of perceiving and experiencing the world with an openness to wonder and multiple perspectives. Activating your Curious Mind opens the doors of perception. It is always the starting point for journeying in the realms of deep imagination.

The Dig: The psychospiritual immersion process of excavating down into the realms of deep imagination, undertaken with Soul Companions. The entry point of the Imagination Matrix, it is a journey offering profound insights.

Earth Quadrant: The first quadrant of the Imagination Matrix, associated with the earth element and regenerative capacities as well as body, deep ecology, self-healing, grounding, the ecosphere, embodiment, soma, the physical, and rhizomatic networks. Element: earth.

Ensouled Stewardship: Cocreation with others at its highest form. Accomplished by tending to the wider ecosystem in collaborative caregiving with the living world, including reaching out to the natural environment (animals, landscapes) as well as the constructed world (buildings, machines), actualized in daily practice and informed by Illuminated Consciousness. See *Imagination-Centered Life*.

Following Curiosity: The capacity to Follow Curiosity invites you into deeper dimensions of awareness. It opens the pathways to the transformative power of the Imagination Matrix.

Four Quadrants: The four dimensions/elements of the Imagination Matrix, including Earth (body), Mind (soul), Machine (procedure), and Universe (cosmic consciousness). Each quadrant has a pulse, a human quality. Each is a field of energy and experience. When these fields are in balance, together they enhance your abilities to heal, innovate, and connect.

Homeplace: The Imaginal hearth where we feel right placed, safe, authentic, and free, with a sense of deep belonging.

Illuminated Consciousness: A state of resonant awareness and immersion in the luminosity and ever-dancing and entwining points of the generative energies found in the realms of deep imagination. Brings a feeling of vibrancy, wisdom, and deep connection, even love, for all beings.

Imaginal: Of the imagination.

Imaginal capacities: Vibrant energies and abilities opened up through engagement with Imaginal fields and figures found in the Imagination Matrix.

Imaginal figures: Characters, settings, and emotions that have embodied Imaginal presence in the Imagination Matrix and exist with archetypal resonance, a collective mythic quality, and an Imaginal life of their own making. See also *Soul Companions.*

Imaginal Healing: When Confluence is attained between elements of the Four Quadrants and the Imagination Matrix System is activated, the possibility for Imaginal Healing occurs. Combined with positive attitude, Supportive Soul Companions, and traditional therapies, the practices of Imaginal Healing contribute to increased functionality, health, happiness, and well-being.

Imaginal Intelligence: The capacity to utilize the insights from the multiplicity of universe-shaping forces, seen and unseen. An expanded imagination generated by the many interconnected points of the Imagination Matrix and enabling creativity, expansion, greater connection, spaciousness, health, and flow.

Imaginal medicine: Imaginal Healing elixirs inspired by the somatic, conceptual, operational, and transpersonal dimensions obtained through Quadrant Work, Soul Companions, and the Imagination Matrix. See *Imaginal Healing.*

Imaginal Play: Kindling fun and joy by Following Curiosity and wonder while engaging with landscapes and figures from the imagination.

Imaginal presence: The felt sense of being in the moment, being both the one and the many, connected to the dimensional nature of all living images and Imaginal experiences.

Imagination-Centered Life: The fulfillment of your highest aspirations when purpose and actions align through Illuminated Consciousness and sustained dedication to cocreation with the wider community for the well-being of the planet through Ensouled Stewardship. See *Ensouled Stewardship.*

Imagination Matrix: The creative force moving through all forms of being. It is ever present and exists below the surface of everyday experience. It contains the interconnected elements of transcendent consciousness of the Four Quadrants: Earth, Mind, Machine, and Universe. The Imagination Matrix exists across multiple dimensions of time and space and generates interactive and interconnected experiences in continuous motion.

Imagination Matrix System: The fourfold system that transmutes the elements of the Four Quadrants so they can be optimized and applied to real-world challenges, personal and professional. Combines cutting-edge research and breakthrough applications from the fields of earth sciences, depth psychology, new technologies, and cosmology.

Innate Genius: The creative force moving within everyone that carries the seeds of your authentic talent and birthright.

IQ4: Imaginal intelligence gleaned through the insights of the Four Quadrants of the Imagination Matrix.

Journeying in the realms of deep imagination: An initiation into another way of seeing, listening, and being. Animated by luminous energies, in this dimension of consciousness the invisibles of psychic reality, our Soul Companions, exist and offer valuable perspectives. See *The Dig*.

Living images: Autonomous embodied images with a life of their own. Vibrant and dimensional beings of the Imaginal realms (creatures, landscapes, emotions, behaviors) often revealed in dreams.

Machine Quadrant: The third quadrant of the Imagination Matrix, associated with operational and procedural insights; generating cocreativity, emergence, and evolution with innovative processes; and the dominion of technology and virtual/augmented/mixed realities. Element: fire.

Mind Quadrant: The second quadrant of the Imagination Matrix consists of the many dominions of the psyche. Multidimensional by nature, the pluralistic mind opens imagination beyond the monovision of the singular viewpoint. Associated with mind/soul consciousness, depth psychology, soul's realization, awakening, and mythology. Element: air.

Mindful meditation: Processes for quieting the body and consciousness through intentional movement, presence, and sound to access and cultivate an inner experience of deep restfulness and transcendence.

Multiplicity: The interconnectivity of multiple perspectives to the interactivity of the bigger picture, the dance of the spheres.

The numinous: First identified by Carl Jung, an Illuminated experience of the mysterious, the unknowable, and a powerful connection to the wholeness of all being.

Poetic expression: Creative expression through writing, drawing, or movement, often inspired by accessing expanded multiple perspectives while in the Imagination Matrix with Illuminated Consciousness.

Rational mind: A mode of linear analytical thinking based on deductive reasoning and singular focus.

Shifting Context: The capacity to change perspective and to move from linear thinking to spatial awareness, from the familiar to the undiscovered. As you do this, you sense yourself becoming a participant in the multiplicity of all being.

Soul Companions: Autonomous Imaginal figures, dynamic inner colleagues/collaborators with whom you cojourney through the Imagination Matrix. Soul Companions can be Supportive or Shadow figures. See also *Imaginal figures*.

State of flow: The energetic force that awakens when the Four Quadrants—Earth, Mind, Machine, and Universe—are in harmonic balance. A uniquely human experience that optimizes our humanity.

Story-Web: The vast interactive network of metapatterns that holds the interconnection of ideas, myths, and dream tellings across space and time, existing behind the veil of the Imagination Matrix and resonating with the sound of the universe.

Theta wave: Higher amplitude brain wave pattern (universal awareness) associated with the imagining mind, Imaginal Healing, and highly creative states.

Universe Quadrant: The Fourth Quadrant of the Imagination Matrix, associated with numinous perception, multiplicity of perspectives, cosmology, transcendent experience, qualities of presence, and spirit. Element: water.

Notes

Introduction: Remembering the Source Code of Imagination

1. Bernadette Duffy, *Supporting Creativity and Imagination in the Early Years*, 2nd ed. (New York: Open University Press/McGraw Hill, 2006); Haneefah Shuaibe-Peters, "Supporting Children's Creative and Artistic Expression from Multiple Perspectives," in *Critical Issues in Infant-Toddler Language Development*, ed. Daniel R. Meier (New York: Routledge, 2022), 122–30.

2. Mirian Vilela, "Chapter III: Earth Charter Dissemination and Endorsements," in *Earth Charter +5 Progress Report*, August 2005, earthcharter.org/wp-content/assets/virtual-library2/images /uploads/Chapter%20III.pdf.

3. UNESCO, *Records of the General Conference, 32nd Session, Paris, 29 September to 17 October 2003*, vol. 1, *Resolutions*, 35, unesdoc .unesco.org/ark:/48223/pf0000133171.

4. Mirian Vilela and Alicia Jimenez (eds.), *Earth Charter, Education, and the Sustainable Development Goal 4.7: Research, Experiences, and Reflections* (San José, Costa Rica: University of Peace Press and Earth Charter International, 2020).

5. Earth Charter International Secretariat, *Earth Charter 2000–2010—Dialogue, Collaboration, and Action for a Sustainable Future: EC+10 Celebrations Report*, 2011, earthcharter.org /wp-content/assets/virtual-library2/images/uploads/EC+10 %20Report.pdf; Earth Charter International Secretariat, *2020 Annual Report: Summary of Activities*, 2020, 5, earthcharter.org /library/2020-eci-annual-report/?doing_wp_cron=1670069286 .9680230617523193359375.

6. Robert Puff, "An Overview of Meditation: Its Origins and Traditions," *Psychology Today* (blog), July 7, 2013, psychologytoday .com/intl/blog/meditation-modern-life/201307/overview -meditation-its-origins-and-traditions; Christine Ma-Kellams, "Cross-Cultural Differences in Somatic Awareness and Interoceptive Accuracy: A Review of the Literature and Directions for Future Research," *Frontiers in Psychology* 5 (December 3, 2014): 1379, doi .org/10.3389/fpsyg.2014.01379; Kaustuv Roy, "Being in Antiquity," in *Education and the Ontological Question: Addressing a Missing Dimension* (New York: Palgrave Macmillan, 2019), 25–80.

7. Emily M. Grossnickle, "Disentangling Curiosity: Dimensionality, Definitions, and Distinctions from Interest in Educational Contexts," *Educational Psychology Review* 28, no. 1 (2016): 23–60; Richard Wiseman and Carolyn Watt, "Experiencing the Impossible and Creativity: A Targeted Literature Review," *PeerJ: Brain, Cognition, and Mental Health* 10 (July 20, 2022): 1–20, doi.org/10.7717/peerj.13755.

8. Joseph Campbell, *The Inner Reaches of Outer Space: Metaphor as Myth and as Religion* (1986; repr., Novato, CA: New World Library, 2002).

Chapter 1: Following Curiosity

1. Madeleine E. Gross, Claire M. Zedelius, and Jonathan W. Schooler, "Cultivating an Understanding of Curiosity as a Seed for Creativity," *Current Opinion in Behavioral Sciences* 35 (2020): 77–82, doi.org/10.1016/j.cobeha.2020.07.015.

2. Nicola S. Schutte and John M. Malouff, "A Meta-Analysis of the Relationship Between Curiosity and Creativity," *Journal of Creative Behavior* 54, no. 4 (2020): 940–47, doi.org/10.1002/jocb.421.

3. Mihaly Csikszentmihalyi, *Flow: The Psychology of Optimal Experience* (New York: HarperCollins eBooks, 2008), loc. 1522; Mihaly Csikszentmihalyi, *Flow and the Foundations of Positive Psychology: The Collected Works of Mihaly Csikszentmihalyi* (New York: Springer, 2014).

4. Edo Shonin and William Van Gordon, "Experiencing the Universal Breath: A Guided Meditation," *Mindfulness* 7, no. 5 (2016): 1243–45, link.springer.com/article/10.1007/s12671-016-0570-4.

5. Meredith L. Antonucci, "Pause, Breathe, and Feel: A Body Psychotherapy Approach to Working with Perseveration," *International Body Psychotherapy Journal* 19, no. 2 (2020): 68, ibpj.org/issues/articles/Meridith%20L.%20Antonucci%20-%20Pause,%20Breathe,%20and%20Feel.pdf.

6. Antonucci, "Pause, Breathe, and Feel," 71–72.

7. Lao Tzu, *Tao Te Ching: A Book About the Way and the Power of the Way*, trans. Ursula K. LeGuin (1997; repr., Boston: Shambhala, 2011), 1–2.

8. James Hillman, *The Force of Character and the Lasting Life* (New York: Ballantine, 2000).

9. Marion Woodman Special Edition Lectures, 2007, Marion Woodman Collection, Opus Archives and Research Center, Santa Barbara, California, opusarchives.org/marion-woodman-collection/.

10. e. e. cummings, excerpt from "i thank You God for most this amazing," in *Xaipe* (New York: Oxford University Press, 1950), 65.

Chapter 2: Journeying in the Realms of Deep Imagination

1. Lynn Kapitan, "Contemplative Art Therapy and Its Trajectory of Awareness, Reinvention, and Critical Reflection," *Art Therapy* 30, no. 4 (2013): 140–41, doi.org/10.1080/07421656.2014.848400.

2. Alfred Korzybski, "A Non-Aristotelian System and Its Necessity for Rigour in Mathematics and Physics," Supplement 3, *Science and Sanity* (Lakeville, CT: International Non-Aristotelian Library Pub. Co., 1933), 747–61.

3. Joseph Campbell with Bill Moyers, *The Power of Myth* (New York: Knopf Doubleday, 1988), 113.

Chapter 3: Soul Companions

1. James Hillman, *Re-Visioning Psychology* (New York: Harper Perennial, 1975).

2. Reshma Shektar, Alex Hankey, and H. R. Nagendra, "First Person Accounts of Yoga Meditation Yield Clues to the Nature of Information in Experience," *Cosmos and History: The Journal of Nature and Social Philosophy* 13, no. 1 (2017): 240–53.

3. Amy Parent, "Research Tales with Txeemsim (Raven, the Trickster)," in *Indigenous Research: Theories, Practices, and*

Relationships, ed. Deborah McGregor, Jean-Paul Restoule, and Rochelle Johnston (Toronto: Canadian Scholars, 2018), 65–79.

4. Australian Institute of Professional Counselors, "What Is Psychological Shadow?," AIPC Article Library, August 19, 2013, aipc.net.au/articles/what-is-psychological-shadow/.

5. Ann Casement, "Encountering the Shadow in Rites of Passage: A Study in Activations," *Journal of Analytical Psychology* 48, no. 1 (2003): 29–46, doi.org/10.1111/1465-5922.t01-2-00002.

6. Charles A. S. Williams, *Chinese Symbolism and Art Motifs: A Comprehensive Handbook on Symbolism in Chinese Art Through the Ages*, 4th ed. (Rutland, Vermont: Tuttle Publishing, 2018), 145–152.

7. David P. Strohecker, "On the Origin of Zombies," *Sociological Images* (blog), The Society Pages, February 17, 2011, thesocietypages.org/socimages/2011/02/17/guest-post-on-the -origin-of-zombies/.

Chapter 4: The Four Quadrants of the Imagination Matrix

1. Kathleen Kuiper, "Ouroboros," in *Encyclopedia Brittanica*, britannica.com/topic/Ouroboros.

2. Helen Schucman and Bill Thetford (eds.), *A Course in Miracles: Combined Volume*, 3rd ed. (Mill Valley, CA: Foundations for Inner Peace, 2007), T-28.II.1: 6–8.

3. Philip Ball, *Patterns in Nature: Why the Natural World Looks the Way It Does* (Chicago: University of Chicago Press, 2016), 78–83.

4. Charlotte Sleigh, "How DNA's Spirals Help Us Understand the Shape of Life," Wellcome Collection, August 24, 2021, wellcomecollection.org/articles/YRaJUhEAADUTzlw7.

5. Karl H. Pribram, "Quantum Holography: Is It Relevant to Brain Function?," *Information Sciences* 115, nos. 1–4 (1998): 97–102, doi.org/10.1016/S0020-0255(98)10082-8.

6. David Bohm, *Wholeness and the Implicate Order* (New York: Routledge, 1980).

7. Stephen Aizenstat, "Holonomic Dream Work" (PhD diss., Fielding Graduate Institute, 1987).

8. Jeanne Sahadi, "Executives Say 'Digital Detox' Retreats Are Key to Their Success," CNN Business, February 8, 2019, cnn.com/2019/02/07/success/digital-detox-executives/index.html.

Chapter 5: Imaginal Intelligence

1. Eberhard Fuchs and Gabriele Flügge, "Adult Neuroplasticity: More Than 40 Years of Research," *Neural Plasticity*, May 4, 2014, article ID 541870, 1–10, doi.org/10.1155/2014/541870; Andrew Octavian Sasmita, Joshua Kuruvilla, and Anna Pick Kiong Ling, "Harnessing Neuroplasticity: Modern Approaches and Clinical Future," *International Journal of Neuroscience* 128, no. 11 (2018): 1061–77.

2. Bahia Guellai, Eszter Somogyi, Rana Esseily, and Adrien Chopin, "Effects of Screen Exposure on Young Children's Cognitive Development: A Review," *Frontiers in Psychology* 13 (2022), doi.org/10.3389/fpsyg.2022.923370.

3. Martijn E. Wokke, K. R. Ridderinkhof, and L. Padding, "Creative Minds Are Out of Control: Mid Frontal Theta and Creative Thinking," bioRxiv (website), July 16, 2018, doi.org/10.1101/370494.

4. Ville Husgafvel, "Meditation in Contemporary Contexts: Current Discussions," in *Routledge Handbook of Yoga and Meditation Studies*, ed. Suzanne Newcombe and Karen O'Brien-Kop (New York: Routledge, 2020), 22–36.

5. Michaela C. Pascoe, David R. Thompson, Zoe M. Jenkins, and Chantal F. Ski, "Mindfulness Mediates the Physiological Markers of Stress: Systematic Review and Meta-Analysis," *Journal of Psychiatric Research* 95 (December 2017): 156–78, doi.org/10 .1016/j.jpsychires.2017.08.004.

6. John Gruzelier, "A Theory of Alpha/Theta Neurofeedback, Creative Performance Enhancement, Long Distance Functional Connectivity, and Psychological Integration," *Cognitive Processing* 10, no. 1 (2009): 101–9.

7. Sima Noohi, Ali Mohammad Miraghaie, Azam Arabi, and Roghieh Nooripour, "Effectiveness of Neuro-Feedback Treatment with Alpha/Theta Method on PTSD Symptoms and Their Executing Function," *Biomedical Research—India* 28, no. 5 (2017): 2019–27.

8. Alex Ni, quoted in "The Divergence Culture," Divergence Neuro Technologies, 2022, divergenceneuro.com/our-culture/.

9. Stephen Aizenstat and Marna Hauk, *Imaginal Intelligence Questionnaire*, 2022, item 8.19, "I sense a generative dynamism below the surface of sense phenomena." (Mean rating was 6.20 out of 7, n = 35.)

Chapter 6: Discovering Your Innate Genius

1. Coleman Barks (trans.), *Rumi: The Book of Love* (New York: HarperCollins, 2003), 123.

2. Michael Meade, *The Genius Myth* (Seattle: Green Fire Press/Mosaic Multicultural Foundation, 2016), chap. 12.

3. "About Fanzhi Zeng," Gagosian Gallery (website), gagosian.com /artists/zeng-fanzhi/.

4. Robert E. Harrist Jr., "Notes on Process," Fanzhi Studio (website), November 21, 2012, fanzhistudio.com/en.php?a=1001&cate= news&name=news_en_5.

5. Maya Angelou (@DrMayaAngelou), "Everything in the universe has a rhythm, everything dances," Twitter, January 21, 2020, 7:31 a.m., twitter.com/drmayaangelou/status/1223267525519204352?lang=en.

6. gatherthewomen, "Jean Houston, Gather the Women," YouTube video, 7:24, September 25, 2008, youtube.com /watch?v=5SQhxMc9DmE.

Chapter 7: Utilizing the Imagination Matrix System

1. Vadim Epstein, "With Human Help, AIs Are Generating a New Aesthetics," *Aeon*, September 22, 2022, aeon.co/videos/with-human -help-ais-are-generating-a-new-aesthetics-the-results-are-trippy.

2. OpenAI, "DALL·E Now Available Without Waitlist," *OpenAI* (blog), September 28, 2022, openai.com/blog/dall-e-now -available-without-waitlist/.

3. Stephen Aizenstat, *Dream Tending: Awakening to the Healing Power of Dreams* (New Orleans: Spring Journal Publications, 2011), 18–21, 185–228; Stephen Aizenstat, "The Living Image," rev., Dream Tending (website), February 2019, dreamtending.com/wp -content/uploads/2019/02/thelivingimage-new.pdf.

4. Stephen Aizenstat, "Illuminating the Numinous Image" (course handout, Dream Tending and Deep Imagination Certificate II Program with Stephen Aizenstat, PhD, 2018).

5. Nele Stinckens, Germain Lietaer, and Mia Leijssen, "Working with the Inner Critic: Process Features and Pathways to Change," *Person-Centered and Experiential Psychotherapies* 12, no.1 (2013): 59–78, doi.org/10.1080/14779757.2013.767747.

Chapter 8: Living the Imagination-Centered Life

1. Heather Murray, "Transactional Analysis: Eric Berne," *Simply Psychology*, September 7, 2021, simplypsychology.org /transactional-analysis-eric-berne.html.

2. Joel Vos and Biljana van Rijn, "The Effectiveness of Transactional Analysis Treatments and Their Predictors: A Systematic Literature Review and Explorative Meta-Analysis," *Journal of Humanistic Psychology*, September 1, 2022, doi.org/10.1177 /00221678221117111.

3. William C. Compton and Edward Hoffman, *Positive Psychology: The Science of Happiness and Flourishing*, 3rd ed. (Los Angeles: Sage Publications, 2019).

4. Karen Lupe, "An Ocean with Many Shores: Indigenous Consciousness and the Thinking Heart," in *Penina Uliuli: Contemporary Challenges in Mental Health for Pacific Peoples*, ed. Philip Culbertson, Margaret Nelson Agee, and Cabrini Ofa Makasiale (Honolulu: University of Hawai'i Press, 2007), 122–35.

5. Daniela Rocha Lopes, Kees van Putten, and Peter Paul Moormann, "The Impact of Parental Styles on the Development of

Psychological Complaints," *European Journal of Psychology* 11, no. 1 (2015): 155–68, doi.org/10.5964/ejop.v11i1.836.

6. James Hillman, *The Soul's Code: In Search of Character and Calling* (New York: Ballantine, 1996), 4–5.

7. Dhruti Bhagat, "The Origins and Practices of: Samhain, Día de los Muertos, and All Saints Day," *Boston Public Library* (blog), October 30, 2018, bpl.org/blogs/post/the-origins-and-practices-of -holidays-samhain-dia-de-los-muertos-and-all-saints-day/.

8. Robert Bly, *Eating the Honey of Words: New and Selected Poems* (New York: Harper Perennial, 2000), 109.

9. Bly, "The Third Body," in *Eating the Honey*, 109.

10. Michael Blanding, "Getting to Eureka!: How Companies Can Promote Creativity," *Working Knowledge* (blog), Harvard Business School, August 22, 2011, hbswk.hbs.edu/item/getting-to-eureka -how-companies-can-promote-creativity.

11. Gregory E. Hitzhusen and Mary Evelyn Tucker, "The Potential of Religion for Earth Stewardship," *Frontiers in Ecology and the Environment* 11, no. 7 (2013): 368–76, doi.org/10.1890/120322.

12. Te Ahukaramū Charles Royal, "Kaitiakitanga: Guardianship and Conservation," *Te Ara: The Encyclopedia of New Zealand*, September 24, 2007, teara.govt.nz/en/kaitiakitanga-guardianship -and-conservation/print.

13. Annaloes Smitsman, "Welcome to EARTHwise Centre: Becoming the Future Humans of an Emerging Planetary Civilization," EARTHwise Centre, 2023, earthwisecentre.org/.

Chapter 9: Imaginal Healing

1. Robert Bosnak, "About the Santa Barbara Healing Sanctuary," Santa Barbara Healing Sanctuary (website), santabarbarahealingsanctuary.com/about-the-santa-barbara -healing-sanctuary/.

2. Elizabeth A. Hoge, Eric Bui, Mihriye Mete, Mary Ann Dutton, Amanda W. Baker, and Naomi M. Simon, "Mindfulness-Based Stress Reduction vs. Escitalopram for the Treatment of Adults with Anxiety Disorders: A Randomized Clinical Trial," *JAMA Psychiatry* 80, no. 1 (2023): 13–21, doi.org/10.1001 /jamapsychiatry.2022.3679; Kevin A. Barrows and Bradly P. Jacobs, "Mind-Body Medicine: An Introduction and Review of the Literature," *Medical Clinics* 86, no. 1 (2002): 11–31; John O. Younge, Rinske A. Gotink, Cristina P. Baena, Jolien W. Roos-Hesselink, and M. G. Myriam Hunink, "Mind-Body Practices for Patients with Cardiac Disease: A Systematic Review and Meta-Analysis," *European Journal of Preventive Cardiology* 22, no. 11 (2015): 1385–98, doi.org/10.1177/2047487314549927.

3. John Gruzelier, "A Theory of Alpha/Theta Neurofeedback, Creative Performance Enhancement, Long Distance Functional Connectivity, and Psychological Integration," *Cognitive Processing* 10, no. 1 (2009): 101–9.

4. Sonya Renee Taylor, *The Body Is Not an Apology: The Power of Radical Self-Love*, 2nd ed. (Oakland, CA: Berrett-Koehler Publishers, 2021).

5. Lori Gentilini Burri, "Relational Somatic Psychotherapy: Integrating Psyche and Soma Through Authentic Relationship" (PhD diss., Pacifica Graduate Institute, 2018), ProQuest 10843840, 13–76; Melanie Starr Costello, *Imagination, Illness,*

*and Injury: Jungian Psychology and the Somatic Dimensions of
Perception* (New York: Routledge, 2013).

6. Ben Colagiuri, Lieven A. Schenk, Michael D. Kessler, Susan G.
Dorsey, and Luana Colloca, "The Placebo Effect: From Concepts
to Genes," *Neuroscience* 307 (2015): 171–90.

7. Kirk I. Erickson, J. David Creswell, Timothy D. Verstynen, and
Peter J. Gianaros, "Health Neuroscience: Defining a New Field,"
Current Directions in Psychological Science 23, no. 6 (2014): 446–53.

Chapter 10: Keeping Our Humanity in a Technological World

1. Rob Patrick, email message to the author, September 15, 2021.

2. David Glen, "Module 3 Talk" (Dream Tending Certificate 2,
2021), 1.

3. Dr. Helen Caldicott (lecture, Los Angeles Children's Hospital,
October 21, 2005).

4. Susanne Röhr, Felix Wittmann, Christoph Engel, Cornelia
Enzenbach, A. Veronica Witte, Arno Villringer, Markus Löffler, and
Steffi G. Riedel-Heller, "Social Factors and the Prevalence of Social
Isolation in a Population-Based Adult Cohort," *Social Psychiatry
and Psychiatric Epidemiology* 57, no. 10 (2022): 1959–68.

5. Eliana Neophytou, Laurie A. Manwell, and Roelof Eikelboom,
"Effects of Excessive Screen Time on Neurodevelopment, Learning,
Memory, Mental Health, and Neurodegeneration: A Scoping
Review," *International Journal of Mental Health and Addiction* 19,
no. 3 (2021): 724–44.

6. Mihaly Csikszentmihalyi, *Flow: The Psychology of Optimal
Experience* (New York: HarperCollins eBooks, 2008); Mihaly

Csikszentmihalyi, *Flow and the Foundations of Positive Psychology: The Collected Works of Mihaly Csikszentmihalyi* (New York: Springer, 2014).

Chapter 11: The Story-Web

1. Joseph Campbell, *The Hero with a Thousand Faces: The Collected Works of Joseph Campbell*, 3rd ed. (Novato, CA: New World Library, 2008), 1.

2. Neil deGrasse Tyson, *Astrophysics for People in a Hurry* (New York: W. W. Norton, 2017), 33.

3. Bill Neidjie, Stephen Davis, and Allan Fox, *Australia's Kakadu Man: Bill Neidjie*, rev. ed. (Darwin, North Territory, Australia: Resource Managers, 1980), 63.

4. S. Prout, "On the Move? Indigenous Temporary Mobility Practices in Australia" (working paper no. 48, Centre for Aboriginal Economic Policy Research, Australian National University College of Arts and Social Sciences, Canberra, 2008).

5. Katarzyna Michalski and Sergiusz Michalski, *Spider* (London: Reaktion Books, 2010). Jeanne Rosier Smith, *Writing Tricksters: Mythic Gambols in American Ethnic Fiction* (1997; repr., Berkeley: University of California Press, 2022), 1.

6. William Shakespeare, *The Tragedy of Hamlet, Prince of Denmark*, ed. Barbara A. Mowat and Paul Werstine (New York: Simon & Schuster, 2012), act 4, scene 5.

7. Jean Houston, "The Emerging Possible" (lecture, Mentors of the Academy of Imaginal Arts and Sciences, March 28, 2022).

8. Karen Barad, *Meeting the Universe Halfway: Quantum Physics and the Entanglement of Matter and Meaning* (Durham, NC: Duke University Press, 2007).

Epilogue: The Pull of the Future

1. "History," Earth Charter International (website), earthcharter.org/about-the-earth-charter/history/?doing_wp_cron=1672850647.7802479267120361328125; Steven C. Rockefeller, "A Visionary Commitment to a Sustainable Future: Mikhail Gorbachev and the Earth Charter," Earth Charter International (website), September 22, 2022, earthcharter.org/a-visionary-commitment-to-a-sustainable-future-mikhail-gorbachev-and-the-earth-charter/?doing_wp_cron=1672843027.3127009868621826171875.

Recommended Reading

Aizenstat, Stephen. *Dream Tending: Awakening to the Healing Power of Dreams*. New Orleans: Spring Journal Publications, 2011.

———. *Dream Tending* (blog). dreamtending.com.

Almansi, Guido. *Theatre of Sleep: An Anthology of Literary Dreams*. London: Picador Books, 1986.

Andrews, Munya. *Journey into Dream Time*. Diamond Creek, Victoria, Australia: Ultimate World Publishing, 2019.

Anzaldúa, Gloria. *Borderlands/La Frontera: The New Mestiza*. 4th ed. San Francisco: Aunt Lute Books, 2012.

Bachelard, Gaston. *Water and Dreams: An Essay on the Imagination of Matter*. Translated by Edith Farrell. Dallas, TX: Dallas Institute of Humanities and Culture, 1999.

Barad, Karen. *Meeting the Universe Halfway: Quantum Physics and the Entanglement of Matter and Meaning*. Durham, NC: Duke University Press, 2007.

Bickel, Barbara. "Socially Engaged Art Education Beyond the Classroom: Napping, Dreaming, and Art Making." *Artizein: Arts and Teaching Journal* 1, no. 1 (November 2015): 79–91. opensiuc .lib.siu.edu/atj/vol1/iss1/12.

Bolen, Jean Shinoda. *Goddesses in Everywoman: Powerful Archetypes in Women's Lives*. New York: Harper, 2014.

Brewster, Fanny. *African Americans and Jungian Psychology: Leaving the Shadows*. New York: Routledge, 2017.

———. *Race and the Unconscious: An Africanist Depth Psychology Perspective on Dreaming*. New York: Routledge, 2023.

brown, adrienne maree. *Holding Change: The Way of Emergent Strategy Facilitation and Mediation*. Emergent Strategy Series 4. Chico, CA: AK Press, 2021.

Cambray, Joseph. *Synchronicity: Nature and Psyche in an Interconnected Universe*. College Station: Texas A&M University Press, 2009.

Corbin, Henry. "Mundis Imaginalis or the Imaginary and the Imaginal." Association des Amis de Henry et Stella Corbin. amiscorbin.com/en/bibliography/mundus-imaginalis-or-the -imaginary-and-the-imaginal/.

Csikszentmihalyi, Mihaly. *Flow and the Foundations of Positive Psychology: The Collected Works of Mihaly Csikszentmihalyi*. New York: Springer, 2014.

Duran, Eduardo. *Healing the Soul Wound: Trauma-Informed Counseling for Indigenous Communities*. 2nd ed. New York: Teacher's College Press, 2019.

Edgar, Iain R. *Guide to Imagework: Imagination-Based Research Methods*. New York: Routledge, 2004.

Fadiman, James, and Jordan Gruber. *Your Symphony of Selves: Discover and Understand More of Who We Are*. Rochester, VT: Park Street Press, 2020.

Freud, Sigmund. *The Standard Edition of the Complete Psychological Works of Sigmund Freud*, vol. 4 (1900), *The Interpretation of Dreams, Part 1*. Edited by James Strachey. London: Hogarth, 1968–74.

———. *The Standard Edition of the Complete Psychological Works of Sigmund Freud*, vol. 5 (1900–1901), *The Interpretation of Dreams, Part 2, and On Dreams*. Edited by James Strachey. London: Hogarth, 1968–74.

Gackenbach, Jane, and Jonathan Bown, eds. *Boundaries of Self and Reality Online: Implications of Digitally Constructed Realities*. San Diego, CA: Academic Press, 2017.

Garfield, Patricia. *Creative Dreaming*. New York: Ballantine, 1985.

Hadfield, J. A. *Dreams and Nightmares*. New York: Penguin, 1973.

Hall, Calvin S. *The Meaning of Dreams*. New York: Dell, 1959.

Harari, Yuval Noah. *Sapiens: A Brief History of Humankind*. London: Vintage Books, 2011.

Hersey, Tricia. *Rest Is Resistance: A Manifesto*. New York: Little, Brown Spark, 2022.

Hillman, James. *The Dream and the Underworld*. New York: Harper Perennial, 1979.

———. *Re-Visioning Psychology*. New York: Harper Perennial, 1975.

————. *The Soul's Code: In Search of Character and Calling.* New York: Ballantine, 1996.

Houston, Jean. *The Possible Human: A Course in Enhancing Your Physical, Mental, and Creative Abilities.* New York: Jeremy P. Tarcher/Putnam, 1982.

Johnson, Robert A. *Inner Work: Using Dreams and Active Imagination for Personal Growth.* San Francisco: HarperSanFrancisco, 1986.

Jung, Carl G. *Man and His Symbols.* Rev. ed. New York: Bantam Books, 2023.

————. *The Red Book: A Reader's Edition.* Translated by M. Kyburz, J. Peck, and S. Shamdasani. Edited by S. Shamdasani. New York: W. W. Norton, 2009.

Krippner, Stanley, ed. *Dreamtime and Dreamwork: Decoding the Language of the Night.* New York: Jeremy P. Tarcher/Putnam, 1990.

Lockhart, Russell Arthur. *Psyche Speaks: A Jungian Approach to Self and World* (Inaugural Series, 1982). Wilmette, IL: Chiron Publications, 1987.

————. *Words as Eggs: Psyche in Language and Clinic.* Everett, WA: Lockhart Press, 2012.

Mahoney, Marie F. *The Meaning in Dreams and Dreaming: The Jungian Viewpoint.* New York: Citadel Press, 1966.

Masters, Robert E. L., and Jean Houston. *Mind Games: The Guide to Inner Space.* 2nd ed. Wheaton, IL: Quest Books, 1998.

Meade, Michael. *The Genius Myth.* Seattle, WA: Green Fire Press/Mosaic Multicultural Foundation, 2016.

Myss, Carolyn. *Archetypes: Who Are You?* Carlsbad, CA: Hay House, 2013.

———. "Sacred Contracts and Your Archetypes." Carolyn Myss (website). myss.com/free-resources/sacred-contracts-and-your -archetypes/.

Nandor, Fodor. *New Approaches to Dream Interpretation*. Whitefish, MT: Literary Licensing, 2011.

Oakes, Maude. *The Stone Speaks: The Memoir of Personal Transformation*. Wilmette, IL: Chiron Publications, 1987.

Park, Coyote, ed. *Behind Shut Eyes: QTBIPOC Dream Anthology*. Brooklyn, NY: GenderFail, 2021.

Signell, Karen. *Wisdom of the Heart: Working With Women's Dreams*. New York: Bantam, 1990.

Somé, Malidoma Patrice. *The Healing Wisdom of Africa: Finding Life Purpose Through Nature, Ritual, and Community*. New York: Jeremy P. Tarcher/Putnam, 1999.

Taylor, Jeremy. *Dream Work: Techniques for Discovering the Creative Power in Dreams*. New York: Paulist Press, 1983.

Ullman, Montague, and Nan Zimmerman. *Working with Dreams*. Routledge Editions, *Sleep and Dreams*, vol. 9. 1979. Reprint, New York: Routledge, 2018.

Watkins, Mary M. *Waking Dreams*. New York: Harper & Row, 1977.

Weaver, Rix. *The Old Wise Woman: A Study of Active Imagination*. Boston, MA: Shambhala, 1991.

Woodman, Marion. *Addiction to Perfection: The Still Unravished Bride*. Toronto: Inner City Books, 1982.

Woodman, Marion, and Elinor Dickson. *Dancing in the Flames: The Dark Goddess and the Transformation of Consciousness.* Boston: Shambhala, 1996.

About the Author

Stephen Aizenstat, Ph.D., is the founder of Pacifica Graduate Institute, Dream Tending, and the Academy of Imagination. He has devoted his life to understanding the profound wisdom and healing power that exist within each of us. His work centers on the insight that, through our dreams and imagination, we can access limitless creativity, innovation, improved relationships, and, ultimately, our human potential.

Such an inquiry was a driving force in his creation of Pacifica Graduate Institute, a center for the study of the human experience through depth psychology, mythology, and the humanities. Surrounded by the beauty of the natural world where the mountains meet the sea, the institute is located on two university campuses in Santa Barbara, California.

Within this setting, Professor Aizenstat pioneered his revolutionary, patented Dream Tending approach, a proven system based on four decades of rigorous scholarship and practical application road tested with students, clients, and global workshops. This approach led to his work on the Imagination Matrix, a new paradigm for thinking more creatively and for living more authentically. Dr. Aizenstat has conducted sold-out dreamwork and imagination seminars, workshops, and pop-up events in the United States, Asia, and Europe.

Professor Aizenstat's methodologies have helped thousands of people to unlock the realms of deep imagination, increase intellectual and emotional bandwidth, and realize personal and professional goals.

Professor Aizenstat has served as an organizational consultant to leading tech companies, international leadership teams, and the Hollywood entertainment industry. He has also lectured extensively around the globe on the experiences of dreams, the Deep Imagination, Imaginal Intelligence, and unleashing your Innate Genius. He is affiliated with the Earth Charter International project through the United Nations, where he has spoken. Professor Aizenstat has collaborated with many notable leaders in the field, including mythologist Joseph Campbell; depth psychologists James Hillman, Marion Woodman, and Robert Johnson; visionary Jean Houston; Chinese Jungian analyst and scholar Professor Heyong Shen; and Aboriginal dreamer and artist Yidumduma Bill Harvey.

Dr. Aizenstat honors his associations with sustainability and seed-saving activist Dr. Vandana Shiva, Aboriginal dreamer Bill Neijdie, and community organizers Dolores Huerta and Cesar Chavez.

For more, visit dreamtending.com.

About Sounds True

Sounds True is a multimedia publisher whose mission is to inspire and support personal transformation and spiritual awakening. Founded in 1985 and located in Boulder, Colorado, we work with many of the leading spiritual teachers, thinkers, healers, and visionary artists of our time. We strive with every title to preserve the essential "living wisdom" of the author or artist. It is our goal to create products that not only provide information to a reader or listener but also embody the quality of a wisdom transmission.

For those seeking genuine transformation, Sounds True is your trusted partner. At SoundsTrue.com you will find a wealth of free resources to support your journey, including exclusive weekly audio interviews, free downloads, interactive learning tools, and other special savings on all our titles.

To learn more, please visit SoundsTrue.com/freegifts or call us toll-free at 800.333.9185.